My Passage to Africa.

Brian C. Rushton.

My Passage to Africa.

By Brian C. Rushton.

Copyright © 2011 Brian C. Rushton.

Kindle paperback edition.

This is my true account of a journey to Africa with two of my friends, Eric (Ed) Williams & Len Hawkins in 1971.

With candid honesty it deals with the hopes, fears, experiences and mistakes of three naïve young men living away from home for the first time. It also provides an insight into the lost world of a bygone era, living with servants, the absurdities of the apartheid regime and the often-farcical workings of a foreign fire brigade.

The world has changed incredibly in the intervening years, so I hope that this tale will interest, amuse & amaze the reader.

Brian Rushton. 2011

Contents.

Chapter 1.

Starting out.

It was in the summer of 1971 when I received an intriguing phone call from two of my circle of friends in Liverpool to say that they had a proposition for me. I arranged to meet Ed and Len at *'The Coach and Horses'* in Woolton village, away from the rest of the gang, where they announced that they were planning an overland trip to southern Africa for a few years. They wanted to see some of the world and needed a third partner to provide financial and physical support, plus a casting vote if and when required.

I was disappointed to hear of their planned disappearance from our social scene, and replied that I was flattered by their invitation but it was totally impracticable for me to accompany them. I owned a wide variety of old vehicles, held a reasonably well paid, steady job -- if mind-numbingly boring -- as a security officer and then there was Monty Python on the TV. I was also worried about finding work abroad despite having experience of several jobs including 5 years with Liverpool Fire Brigade, which had been very poorly paid in those days. Ed and Len were qualified engineers so would easily find work anywhere and I didn't want to be a burden on them. They countered all of my arguments and said that they'd give me a couple of days to think it over before approaching one of the others, but warned that if I didn't go with them I'd regret it for the rest of my life.

My mind was in turmoil as I replayed our discussions while patrolling the deserted and gloomy factory in the small hours of one of the following mornings, when I suddenly realised that I couldn't possibly do this tedious job for the next 40 years like a donkey on its treadmill. As I made my way outside to check the annexes I noticed the first streaks of light in the dark sky heralding the dawn of a normal, routine new day for everyone else, but seemingly to symbolise a whole new life for me. I finished my shift and drove straight around to Ed's house and, over breakfast, told him to count me in.

Fortunately Ed's parents were extremely hospitable and tolerant, so their home was always 'open house' to all and sundry. We always started and terminated our various adventures there because of the unfailingly warm welcome, and the constant supply of tea, coffee, toast and bacon butties. I had no reservations about Ed and Len. A large group of us had toured Europe in our small motor coach for a fortnight in the previous year so I knew them to be amiable, amusing and reliable, yet calm and resourceful in a crisis. Len was generally unflappable with a droll and ironic sense of humour delivered with a deadpan nonchalance; while Ed would frequently launch into one of his hilariously pessimistic and cynical tirades, which veered between irony and biting sarcasm. We were still single and in our mid twenties whilst most of our generation were already settling down with a mortgage, spouse and children, so we were really quite adventurous and unconventional at that time.

My main worry was Ed's habit of regularly bogging his vehicles down to the axles in mud or soft sand, so I knew that spades would be essential items of equipment that we'd need to include but I also feared that there was an awful lot of sand in the Sahara desert where we might be forced to practise our digging and extrication skills. Looking back, if Ed had been quietly planning this expedition for some time, perhaps he'd been sneakily testing our character and ingenuity during our previous trips.

The next 6 weeks were spent in the hectic preparation of our departure. We visited the world-famous Liverpool School of Tropical Medicine for advice on protection against diseases but when they told us of the many injections we should have, my terror of sharp objects almost caused me to abandon the venture right there and then. However, they did give us a lot of vital information such as avoiding swimming in still or stagnant water because of the bilharzia worm which can get into one's blood and liver causing a nasty debilitating illness. We were warned about the tsetse fly, which can cause sleeping sickness (my family suspected that I had already been bitten by a swarm of these anti-social flies). We were also advised to try to avoid being bitten by crocodiles. All sound advice.

We were to use Ed's 5 year old Ford Corsair for the trip, so he and Len fabricated a cow (or camel) fender for it in their lunch breaks, together with shields under the engine and petrol tank to protect them from attack by rocks. We gathered together spades, jerry-cans, numerous essential spares and emergency rations and; because we were non-smokers who ate and drank at a similar, steady rate, could pay for *everything* out of our communal kitty. I worked for a pharmaceutical company so with my staff discount we assembled a comprehensive first-aid kit which included a gross (144) pack of condoms. Len labelled the gross (perversely and paradoxically) as 'the giant economy family-pack' but sadly most of the contents were destined to perish with age. Ah, the optimism of youth!

I sold my Mini, 2 old motorcycles, my shares in the speedboat and small motor coach, but put my beloved Norton motorbike and racing kart into storage to ensure that I wasn't tempted to stay abroad permanently. We set out at the beginning of September 1971 full of excitement and a little trepidation but initially it turned out to be something of a false start. I had my basic 35mm camera with me but Len decided that he wanted to return for his pocket camera after just a few miles, and was shaken to find his mum crying. I was relieved that I hadn't forgotten anything. Ed had acquired visas for all of the many countries we intended to travel through, but we needed to call at the RAC in Croydon to collect a Carnet-de-Passage. Briefly this is a financial bond which guarantees to retrieve a terminally disabled car from a foreign country because of import regulations. However, as we intended to cross the Sahara desert with a 2-wheel drive car they stipulated that we had to freeze £700 in a UK bank account. This was an absolute fortune in those days which we just did not have, so we imposed on the hospitality of my brother in south London whilst we devised an alternative strategy. We were bitterly disappointed to be denied the chance of travelling south through Africa, so the only viable alternative was to hunt around to arrange a sea passage to Cape Town and then drive north. The main passenger fleets were far too expensive, especially for the car, and we would have preferred to drive further south than Southampton. I was beginning to despair and having visions of us slinking back to Liverpool to repossess our old jobs, with the derision of our friends and workmates ringing in our ears. Then someone at one of the travel agents recalled that there was a small Italian line, which sailed infrequently from Italy to Durban and calling in to Barcelona and Cape Town, whose prices were much more affordable. The only snag was that the next realistic sailing from Barcelona wasn't until 15th November. More than 2 months away.

We decided that we would rather 'kick our heels' in the sun instead of London, so set off for Spain. Looking back from the cross-channel ferry to watch the white cliffs fade on the horizon, I silently wondered if this could be the last glimpse of 'Blighty' we might ever see, so couldn't help imagining the thoughts of my father who would have had a similar view as he sailed off to war 30 years previously, when enemies were actively intent on ending his life. In any case, I'd given the others strict instructions that if anything *did* happen to me, my body was definitely not to be *flown* home. I've always been scared of flying.

For driving in France at night, Ed had blanked off the left-dip of the car's headlamps and also fitted stick-on yellow covers, which were merely for courtesy and not compulsory for visitors, but he'd also fitted some powerful spotlights for auxiliary use. However, the yellow covers had quickly disappeared into the weeds, which compelled many impetuous French drivers to register their disapproval with the main beams of their feeble yellow headlamps. They were immediately afforded the benefit of searing white light in equal duration to their protest. Their trunk roads were the dreadfully dangerous single carriageway, three-lane type (as they also were in Britain and other parts of the world at that time) where the faster drivers presumed that the centre lane belonged exclusively to them. We were frequently aghast to witness very high-speed convoys of overtaking and opposing traffic desperately trying to cut back inside to avoid certain death. We usually drove through the night in a rota of driver--sleeper--navigator/spotlights operator, but one evening somewhere in S.W.France we stopped for a meal at a bar/café. The friendly proprietor was keen to practise his English on us (he probably still speaks it with a Scouse accent) so kept buying us beers which at some point were substituted with Pernod. Both he and we were determined to buy the last drink, so inevitably one drink led to another ……………… I cannot remember how the car came to be parked in a farm track overnight, but I vividly recall emerging from my self-induced coma lying on the floor of the car, with the prop-shaft tunnel digging into my side and praying that death would liberate my tortured body from further anguish. I crawled out of the car and on hands & knees grabbed handfuls of grapes from the vines to moisten my arid mouth, muttering those immortal words: "Never again!" Sure enough, to this day I have still never ever touched a single drop ……………

———

of Pernod. We crossed the border into Spain and set up camp at Canet de Mar near Calella on the Costa Dorada, where Ed had camped 6 or 7 years previously with his older brother and some friends with their motorbikes. (I'd also been invited on that occasion but my inherent caution, relative poverty and lack of a sufficiently reliable 'bike had constrained me). Ed was incredulous to see how the explosion of tourism had transformed this region and its people in those few years. The old fishing villages were now modern holiday resorts with nightclubs, discotheques and high-rise hotels. The people were now smartly dressed instead of the drab and shabby clothing that they used to wear; as were the children who had often been barefoot and in rags. The weeks drifted by and we settled into a routine, even picking up enough basic Spanish to be able to do our daily shopping and even joke with the locals in their native tongue. In the evenings we tuned in to Radio Luxembourg for our 'fix' of music. It was extremely crackly and, just like back home, frustratingly faded in and out. Our favourite was Rod Stewart's now classic: *Maggie May*. "Maggie may, but probably won't", we joked ruefully, because the 'permissive sixties' had mostly passed us by. We believed that if it was true that there are 103 men to every 100 women, then we were always the odd three who were left out. In fact Maggie probably *would,* if only we had then known that nice girls need to prove that they aren't 'easy'. In the discos we were able to study at close quarters the 'lesser spotty Spanish Don Juans' in their natural habitat. They were not unlike wolves hunting down their prey. Sometimes alone, sometimes in packs they would prowl about, watching, watching, watching, before moving in for the kill. It seemed to be such a serious business though. They never smiled while stalking, didn't appear to enjoy the music or atmosphere, and rarely -- if ever -- bought themselves a drink. With their swarthy complexion and shirts open to the navel, we were amused to observe that they kept their cigarettes, keys, coins, comb, etc. tucked into their socks to avoid spoiling the line of their ultra-tight trousers. Most of the cafés displayed a sign, which promised that Watney's Red Barrel bitter beer, Typhoo tea and English fish and chips, are served here; which made us realise that the British were then so traditionally habitual that they merely wanted a holiday in Blackpool – but with sunshine. We were sitting in one of these café/bars in one of the narrow shopping streets of Calella one evening when we noticed the sign that proclaimed: 'Heinz Baked Beans served here'.

Ed then wagered that I wouldn't be able to consume a pint of them so, as I'm usually up for a challenge, I accepted, and Ed asked the Spanish proprietor for a half litre glass of beans. The conversation went on for quite a while but briefly it went something like this:-

Spaniard: "Ah, so you want the baked beans on toast?"

Ed: "No toast, just the beans por favor".

Spaniard: "So you want a plate of beans without the toast, Si?"

Ed: "No toast, no plate, no cutlery, just a half litre glass full of beans".

Spaniard: "You want *hot* beans in a glass?"

Ed: "No; cold".

There were now several obstacles for me to overcome: Firstly was the unfamiliar texture of refrigerated baked beans. Next was the etiquette of drinks with lumps in; does one swallow them straight down, or chew? Then there was the reluctance of the beans to leave the tankard, so I had to pour some beer in and swill the mixture around to assist the evacuation. All of this was under the critical gaze of the locals who were shaking their heads in bewilderment at the strange customs of the British.

The highlight of our evening entertainment was each Wednesday in the bar of the hotel across the main road from the site where *The Persuaders* was screened on TV. We enjoyed the action and glamour but the waggish and witty banter between Roger Moore and Tony Curtis was totally lost on us because – bizarrely – it was all dubbed in excitable Spanish voices.

They say that the devil makes work for idle hands. Well he made us buy an electric lamp and 20 metres of cable, which we connected into the base of a lamp-post on the site, covering the cable with leaves. We had to remember to remove the bulb before lighting-up time though because it might have appeared slightly suspicious if our tent had illuminated at the very same instant as the camp's lights.

To keep ourselves busy, we painted the car's roof white to reflect the forthcoming African sun, dug a moat around the tent to take the water from the more frequent storms and made a little bridge into the doorway. Some nights we would lie in our beds listening to the wind whistling through the trees that marked each pitch, fearfully expecting a large branch to crush our tent. We scavenged a large wooden box from the site's rubbish dump, which we appropriated for a table, then cut a hole in the side to house the stray dog we had befriended.

We became quite avid naturalists (not naturists – that's a wholly different ball game) in the studying of our environment. One day we noticed a termite dragging a dead wasp, which was several times its size. We wondered how far the insect had to travel and how it knew the route, so decided to undertake some experiments. I should stress that no creatures were harmed in the course of these tests, and that the wasp was beyond help. With the aid of a leaf we turned the termite around to disorientate him but after running around in circles a few times he set off in the right direction, so we deduced that termites must have some sort of built-in direction finder. Next we lifted the box/table/kennel into its path but he chose the monumental task of dragging his trophy up and over the top instead of making the short detour around it, so we noted that his homing signal must have been much stronger than his sense of logic. Then we confiscated his loot and moved it away to see how long it would take him to find it. We could only guess its gender without the benefit of a microscope, but presumed that he was a hunter/gatherer and fearful of returning home empty-handed as he ran around in panic, even though it was only a few inches away. We concluded that they must have very poor eyesight and sense of smell. Having lost interest long before it reached its destination, we still had to admire its energy, stamina, tenacity and dedication.

We were disgusted by the condition in which some of the campers left the toilets, so we thoroughly cleaned one cubicle and then unscrewed the exterior door-handle to hang in our tent, thus reserving that toilet for our exclusive use. There was then nobody else to blame though.

A section of the site was reserved for self-catering coach holidaymakers in ready-erected tents. As they left for home, these kindly people would bequeath to us the remains of those provisions that Britons abroad cannot live without. Thus our larder contained numerous part used packets of tea-bags, coffee, sugar, bottles of tomato ketchup, HP sauce, and washing-up liquid, many of which we were still using months later in Africa.

As the weather grew colder the holidaymakers drifted away and we met many interesting travellers from a wide variety of countries. Some Australians terrified us with lurid tales of the numerous species of poisonous insects they knew of, and a Canadian couple advised us to run uphill if we were ever chased by a bear. Presumably one would have to come down at some point but apparently bears have trouble with their balance when climbing hills, but will roll downhill and bowl you over. It's worth remembering that, as it could save your life some day. Our advice to them was more mundane, yet probably more practical. Such as: if you're ever in Liverpool, try to avoid slowing your car down too much to prevent your engine and wheels from being stolen; and *never* slam your hotel window, as you'll probably trap someone's fingers and be sued for compensation. (This was long before the stereotype of the thieving Scouse scallywag). Then, if you're ever standing in the middle of 19,999 other people on the Kop behind one of the goals at the Anfield football ground where it was impossible to reach the toilets, ***never*** borrow anyone's rolled-up newspaper, especially if he's drunk 8 pints.

Our tickets for the Italian owned MV *Africa* urged us not to be a 'no-show' so we thought we might as well present ourselves at the Barcelona dockside at the appointed hour.

Ed's mum, next door neighbour, sister and dog
waving us off.

Ed with the stray dog we befriended & Len on the
deserted Spanish campsite.
In the foreground is Ed's exercise wheel, made from
scavenged rubbish.

Ed & Len on the deserted Spanish beach.

Len & Brian out to lunch.

Chapter 2.

We are Sailing.

We boarded the Italian owned ship on 15th November 1971 for the two-week voyage to Cape Town. It was a medium-sized passenger ship whose occupants were mainly from the southern African countries returning home from their travels in Europe.

The weather became noticeably warmer as we sailed south and as we reached the equator the crew held a *'crossing the line'* ceremony around the pool. We were honoured by the presence of King Neptune himself, who bore an uncanny resemblance to the ship's Purser. To be honest his queen was a bit on the butch side and hadn't even bothered to shave. The victims were a couple of extrovert passengers, one of whom was given a 'haircut and shave' by the 'barber' using giant wooden scissors & razor; and the 'surgeon' seemingly removed a string of sausages from inside his patient. There was a lot of shaving foam, ketchup and concoctions from the galley thrown about before the victims were dunked in the pool. They gained swift revenge however by taking most of their tormentors -- and some of the fully clothed officers -- into the pool with them. The king and queen fled.

We flushed numerous gallons of water down the hand basin at this time, to test the theory that if water swirls down the plughole in a clockwise direction in the Northern Hemisphere and anti-clockwise in the Southern Hemisphere, then it must go straight down over the equator. Disappointingly the results proved inconclusive due to the motion of the ship. There was the usual on-board entertainment with dancing to the resident band every night, together with silly party games and competitions. During the day, in exchange for several thousand lire we could have received expert tuition in subjects such as ballroom dancing (but we didn't fancy any of the matrons), clay-pigeon shooting (we didn't like soil-sports (sic), or golfing (we couldn't see the point of learning how to drive a golf ball into the sea), so preferred to ogle the female flesh around the pool. Not that any of them were interested in us, as the younger unattached ladies only had eyes for the Italian crewmen. It could only have been for their uniforms, we concluded.

The more resentful among us dubbed these ladies 'the crew-s***w' but we did achieve a measure of retaliation on them on the night of the beauty contest. We persuaded an elderly, jolly lady to enter, then canvassed the other passengers to vote for her. Of course she won and the young beauties had to applaud her whilst smiling through gritted teeth. The captain was not at all amused as he had to dance with the winner, while his first and second officers had to make do with the two prettiest girls. Our cabin was a four berth with two sets of bunk beds, so we had to share the room with a single young South African long-haired hippy with a wispy beard and body odour, who wore shabby clothes without shoes. He didn't have any money to buy himself a drink so we felt obliged to buy him one each day which he nursed protectively to make it last the whole evening, but he always seemed to be drunk.

We eventually realised that the occasional beer couldn't possibly have produced this effect but it took quite a while for our touching naivete to comprehend that his frequent cigarettes must have contained some exotic substances. Our innocence or ignorance became apparent also, in hindsight, when we were chatted up by some single yet very friendly older women but failed to interpret their amorous signals. What a disappointment we must have been to them, who must have presumed that our masculine mannerisms were completely phoney. We saw schools of dolphins and/or porpoises, pods of whales, and squadrons (?) of flying-fish. We marvelled at the phosphorescence in the seawater that made the spray and foam glow at night, but generally the panorama for hours on end consisted of nothing more than the curvature of the Earth's surface in all directions.

One day the ship's newspaper announced that we would be passing the sister ship MV *Europa* and people actually packed the rails for several hours beforehand just to secure a good view. As the ships approached they turned towards each other, and passed within 50 metres. Well everyone went mad, waving, cheering and whistling. Horns and sirens blared. Numerous items were thrown overboard, including lifebelts and deckchairs. It was truly amazing, but confirmed our view that unless frequent ports-of-call are made, ship cruises are vastly over-rated. Throughout the voyage an extremely friendly and distinguished male passenger had quizzed us -- and some of the others -- about our past, our political views and our plans for the future, but the South Africans on board were very wary of him and convinced that he was employed by their secret police. Were they simply paranoid or just cannily astute? In hindsight, I'd now say that they were probably the latter. At every mealtime we'd been terrorised by our Italian waiter who, with his dapper style and ultra thin moustache resembled a middle-aged gigolo. If we weren't seated at the very start of the meal periods he would make a peculiar clucking noise while waggling a raised index finger sideways like an inverted pendulum; followed by a tapping of his watch. We would very rarely receive the choice of food to which we'd pointed on the menu; and the most timidly apologetic request for a cleaner spoon or fork would trigger an incredible pantomime performance from him. His eyes would roll as his face produced myriad expressions, whilst sighing, huffing & puffing and various other sub-human noises. Remember that this was long before Fawlty Towers on the TV.

We never dared to complain for fear of him coming at us with a carving knife, or having his suicide on our conscience, or at the very least spitting in our food. We did have the last laugh however, when on the final day we left him a derisory 100 lire note (5 pence) for his gratuity, *between us*. I pray that his family can find it in their hearts to forgive us after all this time.

We docked at Cape Town on the penultimate day of November and faced some searching questions from the immigration officers. They particularly wanted to know if we'd ever had links with communist guerrilla groups -- as if we'd have told them had that been the case -- but the only linked communes of gorilla groups we knew of were those in Chester zoo. After the relative luxury of our floating hotel, we resumed our nomadic lifestyle and set up camp in the aptly named Sweet Valley around the back of Table Mountain.

South Africa was a strange country. Everyone was grouped according to his/her ethnic origin i.e. white or non-white. If your distant ancestors had *all* originated in Europe you were classified as white. If one or more of them originated outside Europe you were non-white, which could be sub-divided into African, Coloured (mixed race), or Asian. The whites could also be sub-divided into English speaking and Afrikaans speakers (the Dutch based language) of the Boers. Each group appeared to despise all of the others. We soon noticed that the English speaking whites were the more liberal, and the Afrikaners harsher towards the non-whites. The word 'apartheid' is Afrikaans and this system demanded separate housing districts, hospitals, schools, buses, railway carriages, etc. Even park benches and beaches were marked Whites or Non-Whites. I was surprised that it wasn't illegal for non-whites to trample on the pure white sand of their own beaches.

Every notice had to be written in both

languages, from boxes of matches to road signs. If a roadside information board had the Afrikaans text first we'd usually have passed it before reaching the English section, but the next one would have the English text first just to be fair. It was a land full of immense contrasts: From the prosperity and neatness of the suburbs, to the squalor and litter of the squatter camps. From the wealth of the average white person, to the comparative poverty of the average non-white. From the beauty of the scenery, to the ugliness of their political system. It was also a country of significant contradictions: The South Africans were obsessed with the fear of Communism yet tolerated an extremely authoritarian government. They said that the non-whites were stupid, yet they employed a black African nanny to bring up their children. They said that they were smelly, yet gave the houseboy/maid the run of their house all day whilst they were out at work. They said that they were dirty, yet employed one to handle and cook their food.

The older buildings in Cape Town were a mixture of British and Dutch colonial style but with a strong American influence. In those days we'd never seen shopping malls, hypermarkets, drive-in cinemas, and out-of-town candlelit steak-houses. There was a general feeling of affluence to which Scousers (Liverpudlians) were usually unaccustomed. We drove the 20 miles along the famous Marine Drive to the nature reserve at Cape Point, which Francis Drake called the "fairest cape on Earth". The south-west tip of Africa was a military radar base so it wasn't possible to see the headland closely, but we stood on the high scrubland with the troops of baboons, flocks (?) of ostrich, and herds of wildebeest, and looked south at the merging of two oceans. It was probably a trick of the light but we could clearly see the green of the Indian Ocean to our left and the grey of the Atlantic on the right.

If we'd driven overland as planned we'd probably have settled in Cape Town, but after spending a week in this beautiful area we decided to trek north to see some more of that continent. We folded our tent and headed north east along the superb Garden Route. Stopping at a small town for provisions we heard a commotion on some waste ground and found a group of barefoot black African men and children who were dressed in shabby, faded, ill-fitting clothing which had probably been passed from generation to generation; excitedly chasing a baby wild boar around in circles. Everyone was laughing and shouting, and the piglet was squealing with excitement as it dodged and weaved. We joined the fray and Ed caught it with a flying rugby tackle, handing it over to the grateful locals. We went on our way congratulating each other on our good deed, until it gradually dawned on us (well, me anyway) that they weren't taking it home for its dinner, they were taking it home for *their* dinner! We fell silent for a while, guiltily contemplating our complicity in its grisly fate.

Passing through the Transkei African homeland we noticed that all of the almost naked members of the Xhosa tribe had a full-sized skeleton painted on their bodies, which I learned years later was to celebrate some sort of festival. We hoped that it wasn't war paint but didn't stop to find out. It was here that whilst tuned in to a distant South African radio station we first heard the Benny Hill record *'Ernie – Fastest Milkman in the West'*. Compared with these simple people who appeared to have virtually no possessions, and not even a front door on their mud-huts; suburban Britain with its doorstep milk deliveries suddenly seemed an awfully long way away. After nearly 1,000 miles on the road we booked in to a campsite near Durban to explore the area. It was by far the best site we'd ever known, with landscaped gardens, palm trees, a scrupulously clean toilet block with hot showers, and a beautiful swimming pool. This might seem normal nowadays, but in those days the facilities of most British campsites consisted of nothing more than a field with a water tap fixed to a rotten wooden post in a pond of mud. Often there would be a tiny hut containing a chemical toilet full of a foul-smelling liquid that would splash back viciously if one dropped something into it. You weren't so much getting your own back, as everyone else's. Even our splendid Spanish site boasted only cold showers which were a shock to one's system in the hot climate. A sign on the wonderful beach announced that shark-nets were fitted, but we still preferred the pool for swimming and didn't risk anything above our ankles in the sea, just in case the sharks couldn't read.

Our GB plate seemed to act as a magnet to boorish Boers who were eager to correct any misconceptions we might have about their country. They were quite intimidating in their safari suits with long socks and hairy knees, large frame and height, booming voice, leathery skin and goatee beards but they detailed the compulsory education levels, health-care and subsidised housing for the non-whites. They pointed out that on average their country's black Africans were the wealthiest on the whole continent, which caused a huge problem with illegal immigration. Time and again we heard the same story of a foreign news reporter who showed a group of non-white children a handful of coins. He threw the money into some dustbins and then photographed the children searching for it. The pictures were seen around the world, alleging that they were looking for food.

After relaxing at this famous holiday resort on the Indian Ocean for a few days, we pressed on northwards, passing through Swaziland. All of the roads there were dirt and we thought it was great fun leaving a cloud of dust behind us. We were less amused later when the boot was next opened to find everything, including our clothes *inside* the suitcases, covered in a layer of fine red talcum powder.

The signposting was as primitive as the roads, so on arriving at a border-post; it was no great surprise when they spoke to us in Portuguese. We'd arrived at Mozambique and not South Africa again.

We'd often taken a wrong road before --- but never a wrong country. We decided to carry on rather than go back, despite costing us well over £100 in today's money for visas, road-tax, & insurance, yet we only stayed half a day in what is now Maputo, on the east coast.

We intended to travel through the Kruger Park game reserve which covers an area the size of Wales (why does everywhere have to be compared with Wales?). However, we were told at the entrance that it was compulsory for everyone to be in a secure compound by 6pm for our own safety from the wild animals which were on the loose, or face a hefty financial penalty to pay for an escort. The nearest compound was almost 30 miles away but we had only half an hour to do it. It would just have been possible had there been no unforeseen events, but after the expense of Mozambique we prudently decided to make a very long detour around it. I was driving later that night when the most incredible tropical storm began just after we'd passed the Tropic of Capricorn sign. The road was covered with several inches of water, the rain was bouncing a foot high, the wipers couldn't cope with the deluge cascading onto the windscreen; and I'd certainly have stopped had we seen a lay-by. As the monsoon abated we noticed that the road surface appeared to be moving, and realised that it was covered by a mass of hopping frogs. I managed to get the car horribly sideways on a long left-hander and as my whole life flashed through my mind -- well, the first 6 months anyway -- I remarked how ironic it would have been had we 'croaked' on a carpet of squashed frogs.

When approaching the Rhodesian border in a small town the following evening, we first made the mistake of asking a black African for directions. We repeated this error several times over the next few weeks before realising that Africans, without being malicious, are either too proud or embarrassed to admit ignorance; so will tell you any old rubbish just to spare themselves from humiliation. Anyway, we began to suspect that this was not the main Pretoria to Rhodesia road as it became narrower, but when it disappeared completely knew it definitely wasn't, so parked up for the night. Next morning, as we retraced our wheel tracks, we could see from our compass that we had travelled west for more than 50 miles instead of north. We left South Africa at Messina and crossed the Limpopo River to Rhodesia. Those few hundred yards of no-man's-land separated two very different worlds. We left the stern, hatchet-faced male officials and armed police and were greeted by friendly, attractive young ladies in elegant immigration officer uniforms who spoke only in English and with a much softer accent (they certainly didn't roll their 'R's at us). The police were unarmed, courteous and helpful. In fact, everyone was so pleasant that it was even more of a shock and disappointment to be refused entry into the country.

MV 'Africa'.

Our car boarding the ship.

'Crossing the line'

'Crossing the line' ceremony ended in a free- for- all.

Docking at Cape Town in the shadow of Table Mountain.

Marine Drive between Cape Town and Cape Point.

Cape Point.

Stuck in a mud-hole in Mozambique after Ed had become bored with weaving between them. Seated in the rear without seatbelts, I was almost catapulted through the windscreen.

Dragged out by an exiled British couple.

Raising the dust in Swaziland.

Superb site near Durban.

Broken fan belt near the Drakensberg
mountains.

Chapter 3.

Back into Harness.

We'd been refused entry into Rhodesia (now Zimbabwe) because we weren't carrying sufficient money with us, so could have been a drain on the country's resources. This area of the country at Beitbridge regularly holds the national record for high temperatures and I for one had never known such fierce sun --- hardly the ideal conditions for rational decisions. We huddled into a tiny phone booth for some respite while we decided on a new plan of action. The nearest city with an international bank was Pretoria nearly 300 miles to the south again, so it was back across the Limpopo River to the hatchet-faced immigration interrogators.

"No, we've never been b***** Communists!"
I wondered what would have happened had we
upset them or confessed to a bit of casual terrorising
in our spare time. Would we be condemned to
spend the rest of our lives on this bridge aimlessly
staring into the Limpopo?   We settled into the
excellent yet cheap campsite in Pretoria and cabled
our banks in England for more money. Just our luck
that there happened to be an international monetary
crisis at that time, so we were stuck there for 5 days.
We were reminded that it was nearly Christmas
when walking in the beautiful park adjoining the site
one evening. There were huge illuminated tableaux
of the Nativity with a taped commentary in both
languages alternately, but it seemed totally
inappropriate to hear this gentle tale narrated in the
harsh guttural language of the Afrikaners.

We experienced that same feeling of relief and welcome at the Rhodesian border-post now that we were more affluent, yet the immigration officers didn't even ask to see the money, after all that. We supposed that we'd just been unlucky with our choice of officer on the previous visit, so in hindsight should simply have waited outside for an hour or so before trying again with a more amenable one.

Just north of the border we came to a `Y` junction with a signpost pointing to Salisbury (now Harare) 340 miles to the right, and Bulawayo 190 miles to the left. We were unsure about which road to take as such epoch-making decisions can change the course of history; and because our lives are inextricably interwoven with those of millions of others (either directly or indirectly) merely by being somewhere, or not – as the case might be. So we stood at this crossroad in life for several minutes to take a vote. I'd heard that the second city was a nice friendly place and had procured the phone numbers of two lovely young Bulawayon ladies, who we'd met on the ship. However, Ed and Len logically argued that we'd have to see the capital city at some time so, outvoted, I pointed our wheels towards the north-east and Salisbury. If this momentous decision had been down to `fate` as many would have us believe, why would we have such complicated brains and emotions if our lives were simply following a predetermined path?

Stopping at a filling station for petrol and cold drinks we were amazed to see a huge dying insect feebly waving its legs at the sky. It was about the size of a man's fist and the attendant told us that it was a Christmas beetle, which can usually fly. As this was in the days before the widespread use of full-enclosure crash helmets I shuddered at the thought of being hit in the face by one at high speed on a motorcycle. Len said: "Don't worry. They probably can't ride motorbikes with those little legs".

We came upon a place called Hippo Pools on the main road so stopped to investigate, when a young black African beckoned us to follow him. The twisting path went on for over half a mile and as it wound through some dense jungle, I was starting to feel a little uneasy and half-expecting to be ambushed at any moment. Suddenly we arrived at a large muddy pool where several hippopotami were almost completely submerged. The African made a mating call, at which one of the female hippos opened her huge mouth above the water and replied to him, even though he was obviously not her type. Although neither side had made any mention of payment, I still cringe with embarrassment at the memory of how we merely thanked our new-found-friend for his kindness and drove on our way, not realising that this was our guide's unofficial occupation. It was weeks later when we realised that very few black Africans could afford to do anything for nothing.

We arrived in Salisbury on Christmas Eve 1971, but the decorations of snow scenes etc. In the town centre looked totally incongruous in the searing heat of an African summer. We pitched our tent in the municipal campsite on the city outskirts and met up again with Peter and Georgina, the young English couple who'd travelled overland in their Land Rover who we'd first met in Spain. Small world!   Christmas Day was the strangest we'd ever known. Here we were, living in a tent in a foreign country in sweltering weather, and still in holiday mode. Lunch consisted of bread and cheese and in the evening we fired up our trusty Primus stove to make a pan of chips.   The country had been an illegal regime since 1965 when it had declared itself independent (UDI) from Britain, so was consequently suffering from the economic sanctions that forbade other countries from trading with it. There were plenty of imported goods in the shops but they tended to be extremely expensive due to transportation costs and the various agents' commission. This forced the Rhodesians to develop their own industries instead of relying on imports and we were relieved to read that they'd finally perfected their own cornflakes.   White people in

Rhodesia were classed as Europeans, black people as Africans; then there were classifications for Asians and Coloured people (mixed race). There was plenty of *individual* racial discrimination but far less *official* racial discrimination that we had witnessed in South Africa. Most of this discrimination was of a financial type because black Africans' wages were so low. For example: a hotel owner could *choose* not to serve blacks in his bar, but very few of them could *afford* to drink there anyway and most of the black people would prefer to socialise with their own kind, so the question wouldn't arise. The most incredible example of discrimination was to be found in the cabaret nightclubs though, where all of the black African waiters had to be cleared from the room while the troupes of topless white dancing girls were performing. I never discovered whether this was national law, protection of the girls by the club owners, or on the insistence of the girls themselves.

The large number of very old cars that were in daily use there amazed me, and there were some models that I'd long forgotten. This was partly due to the need to cherish them because of the price and scarcity of new ones and partly because they were resistant to rust in such a dry climate, without salted roads. The interiors suffered very badly though. The plastic grille on the parcel-shelf of our car distorted grotesquely in the heat, it was impossible to grip the steering wheel after parking in the sun, and contact with the vinyl seats could induce third-degree burns to exposed and tender flesh, so we quickly learned from the locals to always park in the shade. Street-sellers constantly tried to sell ornamental dashboard covers to those whose cars had been in the country for some time, so had ugly cracks in their padded vinyl.

Salisbury was known as the City of Flowering Trees for obvious reasons. Many of the roads were lined with mature jacaranda trees that flowered right through the spring months (September --- December) with masses of mauve blooms. Then there were the vivid colours of bougainvillea and many others, which my horticultural ignorance didn't prevent me from appreciating. It certainly was a beautiful city and the inhabitants seemed very friendly, but some of whom were more English than those in England. One such lady was a campsite neighbour of ours who lived with her retired senior military officer husband in a static caravan. She habitually wore expensive clothes, jewellery and cosmetics every day; and spoke with the strangulated vowels and contorted diction of the uppermost English class system which could easily have been confused with a foreign language. Quite evidently, she was not at all happy having three Scousers and their car that was often travelling sideways residing in such close proximity; so she tried to convince us that there was a far superior site on the opposite side of the city. Subtlety was definitely not part of her repertoire, and Ed suspected that she was unfairly blaming us for the drunken singing at 3 a.m. elsewhere on the site. Common as muck we may well have been, but we were still far too polite to enquire why they hadn't availed themselves of that "fah, fah bittah saite on the ather saide of tine".

As every country to the north of here was ruled by a despotic one-party government, we decided that we would look for work immediately to replenish our dwindling financial reserves. I didn't care too much what work I undertook, providing that I could pay for a used motorcycle, my share of rent on a house and a flight ticket home if necessary. When I mentioned the fire brigade as part of my previous experience to the clerk in the employment office, he scribbled on a card and told me to take it to the fire station. After a short interview with a Station Officer, whose only reservation was that as he feared we'd be moving on again before too long; made me promise that I'd stay in the job for at least 18 months, and then instructed me to report for duty on New Year's Day. It really was as simple as that.

On New Year's Eve we headed into town to a nightclub in the city centre. The place was heaving with unattached women, but every time we asked one of them to dance, were firmly rebuffed.

I told Len: "I'll be glad when I've had enough of this". We eventually received the message and retired to our table to lick our metaphorical wounds where we entered into conversation with a fellow Briton. He explained to us that although the time in Rhodesia was physically 2 hours ahead of Britain, effectively it was in fact 50 years behind. Apparently a mutual friend or relative should always introduce a man to a woman. Well that certainly ruled *us* out. Ed was made of sterner stuff or maybe thicker-skinned than we were, but was snubbed over and over again to our constant amusement, until in exasperation he shouted at one startled girl: "Look, I'm only asking you to dance, not to b****y marry you!"

Just after midnight we went out into the street and witnessed some amazing scenes. Cars were being driven about, horns blaring, with more than a dozen people in and all over them. We thought that one car was backfiring until we realised that the driver was firing a pistol into the air. Black and white strangers were shaking each other's hand, seemingly in an act of mutual reconciliation. What a pity it couldn't last! We returned to the camp but stayed up until 2 a.m. to celebrate British New Year and toast our families' health back home.

Salisbury Fire & Ambulance Service was a whole brigade contained in one station. There was a Chief and an Assistant Chief Officer, and each of the two watches (red & blue) boasted a Divisional Officer, 3 Station Officers, 2 Sub Officers, 2 Leading Firemen, about 10 white firemen, and about 20 black firemen. Then on each watch there were 6 white & 20 black African ambulance men. They worked a 24 hours on/ 24 hours off shift system, which totalled 84 hours a week, but to enjoy a whole weekend off it was necessary to work all of Thursday & Friday. A 48-hour shift! The following week would be the opposite of course and we would work the whole of the weekend. The monthly wages were higher than those in British brigades but certainly not on an *hourly* rate. Whites started at $150 (£93) rising to $250 (£155). There was a large turnover of staff because it was the type of job that many unskilled white men tried before moving on to somewhere else. We were also quite a cosmopolitan bunch: Along with the Rhodesians, South Africans, British and Irish, there was one from each of America, Australia, the isles of Jersey and the Seychelles. The Black Africans started on $50 (£31) rising to $100 (£62) per month. A very good wage for the average black man at that time. Also on the station were a Fire Prevention Dept, a workshop with 2 mechanics, and an accounts department because every fire or ambulance call was chargeable. A modest little kitchen fire could set you back several hundred dollars for the fire brigade alone; with a price to be paid for every appliance, every mile travelled, every man, and every piece of equipment used.

I collected my kit from the stores on the station. The fire-kit was the usual for that time, but the undress uniform consisted of loose fitting, short-sleeved safari jackets for summer use, but with the usual blue shirt and black tie for winter. The helmet was in the American style but without the ostentatious badge, but as it was made from lightweight plastic it was like a fancy version of a builder's hard-hat. The metal clasps of the strap would also rattle annoyingly against the shell, so I opted for one of the British, old fashioned, heavy cork ones. The civilian store man was just like every other around the world, jealously guarding his precious stock as if he'd paid for it out of his own pocket. This one even scratched the date of issue on my tin of shoe polish. There was no training school, so training was on an ongoing basis. A man could start at 9 a.m, collect his kit from stores and be riding to a fire or ambulance call at 9.30. The station was 'L' shaped with the white crewmen occupying the front of the top floor in rooms of 4 beds, but the far greater number of black Africans were packed into 2 rooms in the smaller side wing.

I experienced something of a 'baptism of fire' so to speak, for on the night of my second shift, there was a riot in an African township. 'Operation Lockout' immediately came into force; where a steel shutter came down over the main entrance of the station and watch-room window, the side gates were locked, wire-mesh guards were fitted over the windows of the appliances & ambulances, and certain officers were issued with a gun from the station armoury.   I was riding a front-line pumping appliance and our first call was to an overturned van well alight, and from that to a blazing bus. There were bricks and debris all over the road and we had to weave through an obstacle course of wrecked vehicles. Fortunately we only saw the aftermath and none of the rioters, because our driver said that he wasn't going to slow down or stop for *anyone*. (I presumed that this was merely bravado, but when I got to know him better I became absolutely certain that he would have mown them down if necessary as he'd been a mercenary soldier in the Belgian Congo bush war; seemed well acquainted with sudden brutal death, and would often roar like a lion for no apparent reason. He always sat facing me at the mess-room table, choosing to eat his steak completely raw with a sprinkle of salt and pepper but without vegetables, and would gleefully mop up the pool of blood with a slice of bread, smacking his lips noisily).

Next we were sent to a shopping street where every shop was ablaze. What a contrast to my days with Liverpool Fire Brigade where 2 or 3 appliances would attend one small fire in a shop. On this occasion it was one man to 2 or 3 shops well alight, so despite the sporadic lawlessness of my native city, it had never been like this! I was far too busy to even notice the cameraman filming, but my parents recognised me on the BBC TV news, before they'd received my letter telling them that I'd joined this brigade. We received many more calls and no sleep that night, which ironically was the busiest of my 2 years there, but I'd forgotten just how exciting and satisfying it was to be part of a fire brigade, and surprised at how my ingrained training had been reactivated so seamlessly. Ed and Len were offered a two-week engineering contract in the Mozambique port of Beira, more than 300 miles to the east, so we packed up the tent and I moved into the YMCA until they returned. Whilst I was at work they'd bought a scruffy old 600cc Norton motorcycle for me to use, which had seen very many better days and had lost its front mudguard at some point. The petrol tank had been hand-painted in a bilious shade of emerald green, the frame and chrome parts were rusty, the seat cover was split and the engine was leaking almost as much oil as the *Torrey Canyon* (the tanker which had run aground off Land's End a few years previously). We weren't at all surprised that the lights didn't work because the various electrical components of old British 'bikes were always their *Achilles heel*. Oh boy, the previous owner had certainly seen them coming! The lights didn't really bother me too much, apart from the illegality, as my shifts either started or finished at 9 a.m, but when Len found a regular job he had to rush home on the Norton before the onset of darkness. The proximity of Rhodesia to the equator meant that dusk began at around 5 p.m. in the winter and 7p.m. in the summer, so there were no long, light summer evenings. There was another important reason for us to repair the lights: A government campaign was encouraging motorcyclists to use dipped headlights during the hours of daylight to be more conspicuous, but if we were the only ones without them we'd be even more vulnerable. An errant motorist would feel justified in claiming: "I didn't see you, but it was your fault for not using your lights!" I had no helmet or any other protective clothing, which was not much fun at all in that rainy season with the spray from the front wheel constantly in my face and eyes. I didn't yet know my new work colleagues very well, so was also feeling quite lonely living in an alien land with some of the misfits from all over the world who used that YMCA. Not a happy time.

Quite naturally I was very keen to impress my new colleagues, and a chance presented itself late one night when we were called out to a fuel spillage from a railway tanker truck in a goods yard. On arrival our driver realised that he'd brought us to the completely wrong side of this huge yard, so proceeded to perform a 3-point turn. I smartly jumped out of the appliance to watch the manoeuvre from the rear, as per the custom in all British brigades but when it drove away, immediately assumed that they were playing a little joke on the new lad. I waited for them to stop for me a few hundred yards down the road but the appliance just kept on going and I watched the rear lights disappearing in the distance as I stood in the middle of this very dark and quiet road in full fire-kit, with mouth agape. I eventually managed to flag down the only car in that area, whose driver kindly offered to reunite me with my crew although he couldn't contain his mirth at my plight.

"I can't wait to tell this story tomorrow at the

golf club", he choked.   As I told him: "Two questions occur to me.   Firstly, why had nobody noticed my disappearance? Second, if somebody has noticed, have I been reported to have 'jumped ship' and gone AWOL?"   Some weeks later we were called out at about 3 a.m. to a fire in the large Meikles department store in the city centre.   A security guard had noticed some wisps of smoke issuing from a very small open window on the first floor. I was quite slim and athletic in those days, so was chosen to make an entry through this window via the 35' (10m) ladder to open the ground-floor fire-escape door for the crew to access the building. I managed to squeeze through the opening and drop down to the landing of a staircase, but was shocked to find that I was now 6-7 feet (2m) below the window, which meant that there was no way back by this route in an emergency. I pressed on to find the fire-escape, but was dismayed to find that the push-bar had been chained and padlocked, which was perfectly permissible outside of opening hours. I shouted to the waiting crew outside that I'd try to find a door that was only bolted. It suddenly occurred to me what an idiot I'd been to have allowed myself to be flattered into committing several fire brigade sins:-

1. I'd entered a hazardous situation alone.

2. I'd entered an unknown atmosphere without breathing apparatus, although it was often considered as 'sissy' to wear BA unless absolutely necessary – even in Liverpool in those days.

3. I'd gone into a fire empty-handed, apart from a torch.

4. I'd lost my 'means of escape' (escape route)

5. Looking back now, I was also blissfully unaware (as were ALL firemen in every brigade in those days) of the lethal perils of 'flash-overs' and 'back draughts'.

Now here I was; trapped like a lobster in a pot!

My mind wandered back to my service in Liverpool, as it reminded me of a similar incident there in the mid sixties when I was sent for a night shift at the fire station near to Penny Lane which later became famous in the song of the same name. We'd been turned out at silly o'clock in the morning to an arson attack on the local synagogue where the fire was taking hold on the upper gallery. The BA sets we used in those days added oxygen to our recycled stale breath, but these were so laborious and time consuming to clean and service after use that we became unwitting 'smoke eaters', to the detriment of our long term health. The smoke had been so dense inside the building that we could hardly see each other in the dim light from our feeble torches but the four members of our crew had still been sent in to tackle the fire without the aid of BA. We'd been keeping as low as possible to minimise the effects of the heat and the filthy, poisonous, choking smoke but this had become impossible to avoid as we ascended the stone stairs, dragging the heavy line of hose filled with water. Every fibre of our bodies had screamed in protest against the exertion coupled with the deficiency of oxygen; the heat had seared our lungs and throats; tears streamed to flush the irritant from our eyes; and a black-pearl necklace of nasal mucus had adorned the front of each of our tunics. "Lads, lads, wait", the gnarled old Leading Fireman had ordered. We'd all paused expectantly, grateful for some respite from our toil, "I think I can smell something burning", he'd said. We'd all then been rendered completely helpless with hysterical laughter for several minutes, as we contemplated the ridiculous situation in which we'd become embroiled. I had to smile at that memory but this was becoming well past a joke, as the smoke was starting to become extremely irritating, my throat was burning, my eyes streaming; so I realised that in the absence of any support was going to have to find the source of the fire and deal with it. Urgently! I found an extinguisher and – in defiance of all natural instincts

– walked into the thickest of the smoke, where I found a broom cupboard with a couple of smouldering mops standing in a bucket, and quenched them.

My colleagues had been constantly monitoring my progress through the windows and main doors but would have smashed their way in had I been in trouble; so in order to avert the damage that I'd prevented so far, feigned a jaunty nonchalance. The key-holder arrived just as I was thinking that I must have been the only Scouser in the world who was wandering around a shop at that time of night without nefarious intent. As the O i/c (officer-in-charge) inspected the damage for the fire report, I mentioned that as the mops were impregnated with wax polish, the conditions were ideal for the creation of spontaneous combustion but he went for the easier and lazy option of a carelessly discarded cigarette-end; even though he'd failed to find the remains of one.

I was instructed that I shouldn't be too

familiar with my black African colleagues, and not to talk to them as if they were white. I was often taken aback whilst chatting to one of the white firemen, when he would bark an order at a passing black African and then carry on talking in a normal voice. One day we were having a 'question-and-answer-session' during a training period, when one of my white colleagues whispered to me: "What's that gauge called on the side of the T.L. (turntable ladder)?" "An inclinometer" I whispered, in reply. Then when his turn came to pose a question, he asked one of the black firemen: "What is the name of that gauge on the side of the T.L?" "I don't know sir", he replied. "You don't know? You don't bleddy know? It's your bleddy job to know! It's a clinometer (sic). You'd better buck your bleddy ideas up man!" Gobsmacked? I could have swallowed a whole melon.

Most of the black Rhodesians were very childlike in many ways and should *not* be confused with the streetwise African-Caribbeans who we know so well in the UK or USA. They could be kept amused for hours by a simple plastic toy, shrieking with laughter and would accept any amount of verbal abuse from white people, but would very quickly take offence at any real or imagined insult from a fellow black African. They would suddenly squawk like a pair of squabbling birds, but the commotion would end as abruptly as it had begun and without any apparent grudges on either side. They all had a complicated African last name which sometimes looked like a jumble of assorted letters, but usually also with a traditional English one like Jacob, Benjamin or Winston; but often with a strange one such as Sixpence, Yesterday, Careful, or even Nobody. Most of them believed in voodoo magic and would sometimes attend rituals involving the casting of bones and the ritual slaughter of a white bird, usually a chicken. One of the black firemen -- who had seemed to be one of the most intelligent -- refused to be photographed because he believed that his spirit would be trapped inside my camera.

Even the top football-league clubs would usually employ a Muti (medicine) man to cast spells behind the goal to assist their goalkeeper.   They were also very humble and extremely polite, always calling me "Sir" or "Mr Rushton" -- although I never did get used to such deference from people who were sometimes older than my own father. However, an amazing incident occurred one day: I was descending the generously wide main staircase of the fire station when the black assistant of a painter & decorator was ascending.   This hapless man was wide-eyed with fear as I approached, then tried to bury himself into the wall, as if to minimise the slightest chance of impeding my progress.   I just wish I'd had the sharpness of thought to tell him to stand up straight and have some self-respect, but was far too flabbergasted to say anything other than: "Good morning".

Lunch under a huge baobab tree after being refused
entry into Rhodesia, and heading back south again to
Pretoria.

Variation of a zebra-crossing sign in Rhodesia.

The Christmas decorations in Salisbury seemed
incongruous in the heat of an African summer.

Ed on the scruffy old Norton 600 we'd just bought.

Brian aboard 'Old Betsy', a 1926 Morris which was Salisbury's first motor appliance.
Reputedly brought out of retirement to attend a big fire only 6 years previously.

Salisbury fire station. (Appliance doors on the left,
ambulance doors on the right)
The watchroom windows are on the right of the
appliance room doors.

Appliances fitted with riot screens in the fire station.

Some of the vehicles lined up in the station yard.

Chapter 4.

Putting down roots.

We rented a nice furnished flat within walking distance from the town centre but were constantly pestered by black people at the door who wanted to be our cleaner. We eventually employed one and the callers abruptly ceased. The unanswered question is, how did they all know that we didn't already have a cleaner; and then how did the subsequent ones know when we did have one?

We became quite friendly with Martin, a young Rhodesian from a neighbouring block of flats who owned a 650cc BSA motorcycle. One Saturday morning he offered to take us for a drink at his sports club some 10 miles out of town near the airport. I was nominated to pilot the Norton because I'd had the most experience of it. Ed quickly jumped up behind Martin, leaving Len with the Norton pillion. Remember that we still had no proper clothing; our bike had no front mudguard or lights and was not exactly equipped with sporting tyres. Nevertheless, after just a few miles it became obvious that Martin was intent on leaving us behind. Now, many motorcyclists are competitive so I wasn't going to let him get away that easily; but most white Rhodesians also had a fiercely competitive patriotism, believing that their country had been cornered into independence and then abandoned by the UK. This patriotic pride manifested itself while we were having a drink, or two, on the club's veranda. Martin gave each of us a cricket ball and challenged us to throw it as far as we could manage across the playing field. I was pleased that mine was the furthest until he tossed one to a carefully chosen club member who hurled it almost twice the distance of my quite impressive effort. Rhodesia 1 -- UK nil.   As we set off on the return journey with Ed on the Norton pillion this time, I shouted: "Take it easy eh, Mart. We haven't got helmets like you". He must have seen this as some sort of weakness as he seemed to go even faster.   I'd once trained as a despatch rider at the Fire Services' College at Moreton-in-Marsh, escorting convoys of 'Green Goddess' fire appliances and supporting vehicles in the days when we were all in fear of nuclear war. Therefore I was well aware that any following vehicles have to drive faster than the ones ahead due to the 'caterpillar effect'; but with some encouraging noises from Ed I just about managed to stay in touch. We roared through the town centre with footrests scraping the road on every corner. Martin and Len went through a set of lights on amber and I was just about to follow when I noticed the police car behind, so slammed on the brakes but stopping just over the white line. 2 – 0 to Rhodesia!

We sat there in an incriminating cloud of thick blue smoke from an oil leak onto a very hot engine, which ticked and clicked as the various components expanded or contracted. To the policemen's inquisition of who we were chasing, truthfullyish replied that we were new here and then lied: "So we've never seen them before in our lives".

I can't remember if I played 'the fire brigade card' but was fined $20 for (technically) failing to stop at a red light, although the charge sheet could and should have included speeding and reckless driving, plus the numerous defects of the bike, so I got off extremely lightly. However, the fine was about half my weekly wage which I could ill-afford at that time so argued that it should be paid out of our communal kitty because it could just as easily have been either of the other two who was driving, but they rightly claimed to be merely passengers.

Next, we purchased a newish 3 cylinder 500cc Kawasaki motorcycle which was so suicidally fast we nicknamed it *The Kamikaze*. The Norton had been fast and powerful in its day but these new breeds of Japanese two-strokes were phenomenal! Ours was reputedly the fastest of only 5 in the country, after having had the power increased & the gearing raised by a local engine tuner, so it could easily lift the front wheel when accelerating – even in top gear at over the 'ton'. We subsequently discovered that this local god had 'feet of clay' when the middle cylinder seized due to his having inadvertently and carelessly blocked the oil-feed hole with gasket cement, and he hadn't even bothered to match-up the ports in the pistons with those in the cylinders.

The open roads there were fantastic with little traffic, no speed limit, long straights and – mostly -- gentle sweeping bends so it was possible to *average* 100+mph; but with the wisdom and caution of age, I can now see that I must have had rocks in my head to use those sort of speeds on those

———

particular roads. It would only have needed one of the many cycling black Africans to have turned across my path, or an antelope or other wild animal to have run across the road for it all to have ended in a very gory and painful heap. As things were, it was frightening how quickly I closed up behind the huge lumbering lorries which often towed double trailers, but the most obvious drawback of using that speed was the petrol disappearing at a ludicrous 20mpg; so we used to say that Kawasakis could pass *anything* on the road *except* a filling station. The petrol stations were only ever in towns, which were sometimes 100 miles apart, so a long journey had to be planned very carefully and the cruising speed adjusted accordingly, so that our paltry 3 gallons didn't run out prematurely. The fuel disappeared at such an alarming rate; I jokingly suggested that we widen the air vent hole in the petrol tank-cap to prevent a vacuum from occurring.

Then I bought an Austin 1800 car, which were universally known as 'land crabs' for some reason. It was like a grossly obese Mini but with twice the engine size, which afforded effortless cruising. I don't know why we didn't pay for it out of the kitty as we did with both of the bikes, because we all shared the four vehicles. Len usually had the first choice because he started work the earliest.

They had no equivalent of our MoT test there, so nobody seemed concerned that both front tyres of the Austin were as bald and smooth as billiard balls. The cost of imported tyres was prohibitive so most people used remoulds which I'd never ever done in the UK, but my work colleagues assured me that the locally made ones were easily as good as new tyres. I was extremely sceptical because of the hot climate and the high cruising speeds that were possible, but reluctantly bought a pair.

We'd been given an old 'pudding basin' helmet by this time but fancied one of the full-enclosure ones which were a fairly new style even in the UK and USA in those days, and also needed some engine spares, tyres, and a mudguard for the Norton. Len wasn't yet eligible to take any time off from his new job, so Ed and I decided to make the 1500 mile round trip to Johannesburg (Jo'burg or Joey's to the locals) with our extensive shopping list, plus some requested items for our workmates. We had enough money to pay for this lot but were officially only allowed to spend $80 *between us* due to the Exchange Control Regulations, so were advised to ask each shop for a 'Rhodesian receipt', which would be fully itemised but marked at about half the true price that we'd paid.

We were only about an hour south of Salisbury and bowling along at 85-90mph when a tremendous thumping noise set in with a corresponding shake in the steering. Ed, who'd worked at the Dunlop factory with Len in Liverpool, inspected the front tyres and said: "It's a classic case of AUT in the front offside".

"Eh? What's that?"

"Air under tread", he replied.

So much for local remoulds!   My annoyance was tempered with relief that it wasn't anything more serious. We changed the wheel and proceeded a little more sedately, but travelled only about another hour before running out of petrol, learning that when this particular gauge showed that it was empty it literally *meant* that it was empty, dry, and totally bereft of fuel. We knew that there wasn't a filling station behind us within 100 miles, so Ed hitched a lift onwards where there was one, fortunately only about 10 miles away. We ensured that we kept our new can brim-full of petrol for future emergencies.

For a couple of nights we slept on the floor of an apartment belonging to a mate in Jo'burg who we'd met on the ship, whilst we completed our shopping which now also included a decent tyre for the Austin. The shopkeepers must have had plenty of Rhodesian customers because they all gave us two receipts without our requesting them. One for us and an itemised one for the Rhodesian customs, which totalled about $70 even though we'd spent well in excess of 200.   We'd allowed ourselves an average of 60mph for the return journey in order to reach the border post before it closed at 8pm, if we didn't want to spend an uncomfortable and boring night sleeping in the car for 12 hours, and were comfortably on schedule when the fan belt broke. We limped the 15 miles into Pietersburg with the engine boiling and the radiator snorting like a steam engine.   Buying the one which the Austin manual in a garage stated was correct; we found it was far too short. Now it was a matter of trial and error, with one of us feverishly fitting the belt from the top while the other crawled underneath with a spanner to adjust the position of the alternator to tension the belt. We must have tried at least a dozen before finding the correct size, and it transpired that the serial number of the belt had been misprinted by just one of the several digits, so owners of this model must have been having the same problem all over the world. It was now dark and we still had about 150 miles to go in just over 2 hours. It was like *The Wacky Races* but we arrived with literally a couple of minutes to spare and, as we'd hoped, they didn't notice the new tyre that we were smuggling in on one of the rear wheels; probably because it was in the dark and right at the end of a long day. We still had to navigate almost 400 miles before reaching the comfort and sanctuary of our beds after a very stressful, tiring day but these miles were quickly reeled off in such a comfortable, spacious and effortless car.

A few months later we moved into a beautiful, furnished, spacious, Dutch-colonial style bungalow set in a huge garden. We'd kept in touch with Peter and Georgina -- the young English couple who we'd met in Spain when they were travelling overland -- and they agreed to share the house rental with us. With the house, we inherited 2 Alsatian guard-dogs that roamed the garden and, like most of the Rhodesian dogs they were naturally racist. I was assured that it wasn't as a result of training that they would welcome any white burglar with a damned good licking, but would attack every innocent black tradesman who they didn't know. The black postman had to leave our mail under a rock just outside the gate.

We weren't very adept at housework especially in such a large house, and our culinary expertise was fairly limited, so we decided to employ a house-boy. We had a succession of dreadful ones who were nothing but trouble and who'd destroyed our food in their attempts at cooking; or stolen various items of clothing and toiletries. Even Georgina noticed that items of her underwear were gradually disappearing during our employment of one man. That particular house-boy must surely have been a pervert because he couldn't have sold her smalls, and they definitely wouldn't have fitted either of his wives. George was tall, elegant and slender, whereas black African women believed that to be short, stocky and plump was to be strong, healthy and attractive.

Every black African employee had to be in possession of a government identification booklet which contained his/her photograph, with full name, etc. to prove that they weren't illegal immigrants, together with a section where previous employers could leave their comments. In this way an unscrupulous or vindictive employer could easily wreck a former employee's chances of finding another job. However, we couldn't prove any allegations of dishonesty or incompetence, but at the same time we had the responsibility of warning any future employers, so our references for the dodgy ones were ambiguous, neutral, or with grudgingly faint praise. Then we hit the jackpot with Lewis, our elderly house-`boy` who lived in a tiny 2-roomed house called a kias (pronounced kyah) in the garden behind our house during the week, but went home to his family in one of the townships each weekend. Lewis was superb in performing all of the household tasks of our mothers, apart from kissing us goodnight. He even ironed our socks with the top halves turned inside out to make dressing easier for us. (Actually it was essential to iron *all* laundry thoroughly because of the putsi flies that lay their eggs in drying clothes. These eggs could somehow burrow into the wearer's skin and cause a painful boil-like sore that housed a number of maggots). Lewis was very camera shy but I'd certainly have taken a sneaky photograph of him had I known I was to write this book.   He was a cross between butler, cook, housekeeper, waiter, and friendly adviser. We felt like kings each morning, sitting down to a beautifully laid table with full English breakfast instead of our more customary bite of toast on the run.   As I have said, Lewis was wonderful as a housekeeper but he was not so good with 'modern' technology.   He polished our pans until they gleamed. Unfortunately for us he'd never heard of Teflon coatings.   Then one morning, one of my work colleagues had reason to phone me, and the conversation with Lewis went like this:

"Can I speak to the boss please?"

"I'm sorry sir; they are all out at work".

As we'd just come off duty, my colleague wondered if he had the wrong number, so he asked: "What number is that?"

"Number 36 sir".

"No, not the house number. What is the phone number?"

"I do not know sir".

"Listen, if you look at the dial you will see a number on it. Can you read it out to me?"

"Oh yes sir.   0 ---- 9 ---- 8 ---- 7 ---- 6 ---- 5 ---- 4 ---- 3 ---- 2 ---- 1"

We asked around to see what the going rate of pay was for a house-boy, and it varied between $10-$16 per week. We paid Lewis $20 per week due to a mixture of naiveté, embarrassment, gratefulness and British fair play but mainly because 20 is easily divisible by 5, and he was so much better than the useless ones we'd employed previously. We also provided his food, which was usually stewing-beef, corn-on-the-cob, and ground maize sadza (a kind of thick porridge that they rolled into balls between their palms) and was the black Africans' staple diet.

We had neither the time nor inclination to maintain such a huge garden, so also employed a young gardener, Kenneth, who was paid only $10 a week partly due to his youth but mainly because he was incapable of original thought and no more of a gardener than would a lighthouse keeper be one. One weekend we noticed that he was hosing the garden in the heat of the midday sun, so Peter -- easily the most masterful of us -- went out to tell him that he must only water the garden at 6 o'clock each day. Then as an afterthought said: "Oh, and will you clean up the dog-dirt from here, here, there, there and there please?"

Shortly after 6pm, we looked out and there was Kenneth spraying one of the piles of excrement with water. Ed wondered if he thought that it was a lava tree. Peter went out to speak to our supposed gardener and the conversation went thus:

"Do you understand English Kenneth?"

"Yes boss".

"So what must you do at 6 o'clock?"

"I don't know boss".

"Look Kenneth, if you don't understand what I say you must tell me. OK?"

"Yes boss."

"So what did I just say?"

"I don't know boss."

Peter then spent the next half-hour demonstrating to him how to water the massive garden. Hmmmm! Perhaps Kenneth was not so daft after all.   The following evening there was a tremendous tropical storm and ---- you're ahead of me here aren't you?   Yes, there was Kenneth, drenched to the skin but obediently spraying the flowerbeds.   It was strictly illegal for South Africans to have sexual relations with those of a different racial colour but some men habitually bent the law by spending weekends in the protectorate countries of Lesotho and Swaziland for this purpose. I suppose that the possibility of mixed-race children resulting from such dalliances would have made the control of segregation much more difficult in apartheid South Africa. I know not whether money changed hands on a professional basis, or whether the men merely took advantage of those unsophisticated and vulnerable women. Such liaisons were not illegal in the more liberal Rhodesia but they were heavily frowned upon – yet not infrequent. One of my work colleagues was taken in to hospital for a major operation, and I wanted to visit him one day on our day off. Another of my colleagues (who I shall call Rod to protect his identity) declined my offer of a lift on the pillion of the Kawasaki and collected me from home in his car. As we drove along he wondered if the patient's wife would need a lift there as she couldn't drive, so we called in to their house. The house-girl told us that the madam had just left for the hospital by taxi so we returned to the car where Rod said: "Just wait here for a few minutes while I check something out", and he walked back to the house. I sat in his scorching car for about 15 minutes before becoming anxious about the time, so went to investigate. Hearing some noises from the open window of the ground-floor bathroom, I was astounded to see Rod having sex with the house-girl against the wall. When I quizzed him later, he admitted that he'd paid her a couple of dollars but I didn't like to ask if that sum had been negotiated to supplement her meagre salary, or if it was a bribe to keep her quiet. I suppose it could be said that Rod did have the decency not to use his friend's bed, or indeed his wife!

Our flat with Ed on the balcony.

View from our flat, with our pal Martin's BSA outside his flat.

Austin 1800 out of petrol, miles from anywhere.

The spacious, luxury house we were renting, set in huge gardens.

The roads were fantastic.

On the left can be seen one of the old rural 'strip' roads where passing traffic would place two of their wheels on the tarmac and two on the dirt. Some were still of loose gravel.

Rider's eye view of the fabulous roads.

Brian with the 500cc Kawasaki.

The renovated Norton with Len's girlfriend's servants
& Brian.

Cecil Square in Salisbury centre, with the Meikles
hotel in the background. (See Epilogue).

Suburban road with the jacaranda trees in flower.

Chapter 5.

Promotion......... but at a price.

Salisbury Fire & Ambulance Service attended about 1,500 fire calls a year and probably 10 times this amount to ambulance calls. Most of the fires involved grass, with the usual mix of house & car fires, industrial incidents and traffic accidents, but very few malicious false alarms.

Prior to 1970 the brigade would only turn out to calls inside the city boundary. This was all to change when a householder phoned to report a fire in his home, but was told by the watch room man (switchboard operator) that unfortunately his address was outside the station area, so we couldn't attend. He phoned again later, begging for assistance and was put through to a Stn. O (station officer) who told him that he was sorry but there was nothing we could do. Again he phoned, demanding to speak to the CFO (chief fire officer) who reluctantly agreed to send an appliance but which, by then, could only damp-down the smouldering foundations. This now homeless ex-householder turned out to be an MP who caused such a fuss that thereafter the boundary was increased to cover the Greater Salisbury area, with discretion to go further. Before these changes the ambulances were crewed by firemen with no specialist skills, but were then designated as ambulance drivers (A/Ds) and trained in casualty-handling, first-aid, oxygen therapy, etc.

Firemen were still used in times of crisis however, and I attended several ambulance 'shouts' in my time there.

Casualties who used the ambulances were also charged. Black Africans paid $1 per journey, while white people were charged 50 cents *per mile*, from the fire station to the scene, to the hospital, and back to the station. It would have been far cheaper to call a taxi, as they don't expect you to pay from and to their own depot.

The newest ambulances (Nos.11 & 12) were a Japanese make and reserved for white European, Asian, and mixed-race casualties, and crewed only by white crews, because white casualties wouldn't want to be indebted to black people especially when at their most vulnerable. These two ambulances were always kept on standby even when all of the others were in use.

Nos. 9 & 10 were American Chevrolets and used for blacks *or* whites with the appropriate crews.

Nos. 1 -- 8 were the oldest and most unreliable, converted from British vans (2 each of Commer, Standard, Morris and Ford), and used for black casualties with black African crews.

The crews would moan on their return if sent to transport a patient of the 'wrong' colour, but would never leave him/her at the side of the road as was the case, apparently, in South Africa. The watch room man needed to ask the caller whether a European or African ambulance was required. There were three hospitals in the city: Salisbury General for the white patients, *Princess Margaret* hospital for Coloured (mixed race) patients, and Harare (then the largest of the African townships) hospital for the black Africans, which was reputedly the most modern and best-equipped in that whole continent. One day 3 of the European crews turned out to an overturned army lorry and transported some badly injured soldiers to Salisbury General. They were inspected, thought to be black Africans and sent on to Harare where again they were assessed, correctly classified as Coloured and sent to the `Princess Margaret`. What a way to treat injured people!

The black Africans received free medical treatment at their superb hospital, whereas the whites, Asians and mixed race folk had to pay for medical insurance. I gashed a finger badly at work one day and sampled at first (bloodied) hand the services of one of our ambulances. Whilst waiting to be attended to at casualty, I had to complete a long and complicated form with all of my personal details & insurance, despite leaking blood and weak from shock & pain. I saw one unfortunate man trying to fill-in his form lying flat on his back on a trolley. Obviously, if one were unconscious or very badly injured he/she would still have received the necessary initial treatment, but this incident certainly made me fully appreciate our over-stretched, long-suffering, and much-derided British NHS.

Watch room duty was a four-hour nightmare. It was also a frequently recurring nightmare because it was only performed by white Europeans and requiring six of us in a 24-hour shift. The huge console resembled the flight deck of an airliner with its flashing lights, buzzers and bells. There was an extremely complicated switchboard, a microphone for each of the fire and ambulance radio systems and one for the Tannoy, a phone to receive fire calls; and no less than 5 for ambulance calls, all of which could have rung simultaneously. I argued that it would be more logical to have only one, as callers would be more understanding if they received an engaged tone rather than a constantly ringing one; and far better for the operator taking details of a call not to have constant ringing in his other ear. There was a ledger on the massive desk in which every detail of the numerous changes or movements of personnel or vehicles had to be recorded in longhand using *blue* ink. Ambulance calls were logged in *black* ink and fires in *red.* It was normal to fill at least 8 pages in one stint.   Operators also collected the $1 payments for black African calls, usually in small change, record the details in the receipt book and deposit the money in a safe.   There were also constant interruptions at the foyer window from black people enquiring if we had a vacancy for a 'fire extinguisher'.   One of these callers set-off the fire alarm by intentionally breaking the glass of the call point in the foyer, just to make such an enquiry. The chances of a job were very low anyway, but in his case they were way below zero.   We had a small shop on the station which was opened at certain times of the day by one of the officers to sell sweets, crisps and soft drinks but for a special occasion such as a birthday or leaving 'do' we'd need something stronger for a dormitory party in the evening. The watch room man would log a spurious ambulance call to the town centre, where the crew would take a stretcher into the storeroom of a liquor store with whom we had an 'arrangement'. They would load 3 or 4 crates of beer onto the stretcher, cover them with blankets, and carry it to the ambulance through the gawping pedestrians who would often be seen to doff their hats and 'cross' themselves in respect. The crew would then radio in that it was a false-alarm, but the watch room man had to remember not to send the ambulance somewhere else until the phantom patient had been unloaded at the station.

There were no black officers in those days because the whites wouldn't have accepted orders from them. I never felt that the quantity of melanin in my skin was sufficient qualification for me to give orders to black Africans of the same rank, although my white colleagues suffered no such reservations. So even though I have never craved promotion, I sat the Leading Firemen's exam which supposedly sorts out the sheep from the goats -- or the Serb from the Croats, as we'd say nowadays. The format of the exam followed the British style at the time, of English, maths and general knowledge. I know that it is fashionable nowadays for fire fighters to scoff that general knowledge is irrelevant to the fire brigade. I disagree. General knowledge and wisdom usually develop with age and experience and these cannot be found in books. So this system did have the benefit of excluding those with a photographic memory of the manuals but who were not worldly-wise or experienced. For example, I knew from my travels that Venice was in Italy yet one unworldly young Rhodesian chose Spain for his answer; while another thought it was in Chile. The second part of the exam was to take control of fire drills (pretend fires) and practical tests much as it is today, and I managed to pass it. Flushed with success, I then sat the first part of the Sub Officers' exam, which was all based on the fire brigade manuals. To say that the subsequent practical part was a debacle would be like describing the Great Fire of London as 'a bit of a bonfire'. Firstly I was detailed to give a lecture on the old-fashioned oxygen BA (breathing apparatus) sets which had long been superseded with modern compressed air ones. I'd had experience of these old sets but most of my audience had never ever seen one as they were designed and made long before any of us were born. One of the officers had drawn a sketch of one on the blackboard from a photograph in the manuals for me to explain the workings and features. Anyway, I entered the lecture room to be met by a sea of mainly black faces staring at me expectantly, and it was all going reasonably well until my several attempts at humour fell totally flat for whatever reason, and it quickly descended into a downward spiral of chaotic calamity. My confidence was shaken, so I started talking nonsense: "This is the nose-clip, which fits …….. er …….. on the nose, and these are the goggles which …… er …… should be worn". The worse it went, the worse it went, until eventually, I was a gibbering wreck. "This is the absorbent which filters the carbon monoxide ….. er ….. I mean carbon dioxide out of our exhaled breath, and is made from calcium chloride …….. er ………no it's not, that's the coolant ……… er ……… no it's not, ….. yes it is. Well it's one of those anyway!" When I asked if there were any questions, I certainly didn't expect someone to ask me: "What is your favourite colour, Sir?" I was so mentally scarred by this traumatic experience that I've never been able to conduct a lecture ever since.

The combination drill (where two crews work in conjunction at a larger pretend incident) was just as bad. It was deemed to be a 'dry-drill' (to conserve precious water during that period of serious drought) where we had to imagine that we were indeed using water; but with numerous hoses scattered around the yard like spaghetti it was difficult for us (but not the judging panel!) to remember which ones were and weren't supposed to be containing water. Men were uncoupling hoses that were supposed to be under pressure and one man did physically and erroneously open the hydrant to charge a hose which wasn't manned or connected. The hose reared up like a giant snake spitting venom, with the head flailing about menacingly. There was so much going wrong that I totally lost control of it, and it culminated when the most senior officer was forced to step in to halt a dangerous situation whilst I was pointing out to the other crew that the ladder they were trying to extend was upside-down. Obviously I failed that exam, but *was* promoted to Lfm.(Leading Fireman).   This was not quite as good as it sounded: For the extra few dollars a week we were expected to set a good example (this didn't suit me at all as I was essentially one of the lads); be called out at all hours to dispense fuel to the ambulances and appliances, then complete the paperwork; still perform watch room duties (aaarrgghhh!!) and ride as O i/c (officer in charge) of the 3rd or 4th pumping appliance. We also had to spend a day or night as the only white man, in charge of one the two new stations that had just been opened in the suburbs; and complete 'fire-report' forms.   These   fire-reports could be horrendous, with the usual questions as to the cause of the fire and damage etc, with space for a drawing with all of the measurements, and precise details of the owner to whom the bill would be sent. A simple grass fire on one of the many pieces of open land in the city would require a trip in a pick-up truck -- when time permitted -- to the council planning department to study their maps. To our dismay we would then find that this innocuous piece of land was designated as a future housing estate and owned by hundreds of people. Apart from the house plots, the planned roads belonged to the Highways Dept, the verges to Parks & Gardens, the footpaths to Amenities, then there were the service utilities, etc, etc, etc. The bill was apportioned and sent out to each of them. Usually someone would dispute that the fire had affected his/her land, requiring another trip to the fireground for measurements, by which time the grass had sprung up again.

Another regular occurrence for us was the dealing with vehicle fuel spillages. Drivers would often fill their tank to the brim, then park on the steeply cambered streets in the town centre where the petrol would seep past a loose filler-cap to form a hazardous pool under the vehicle, so we'd be called upon to take a pick-up truck with a pile of sand to spread on it. Whilst recording the details, it was vital (but surprisingly necessary) to keep one eye on my colleague to ensure that he didn't create a spark with the shovel. The bill, which the driver would consequently receive for the two of us to travel out there, would prove that it was a very costly and careless mistake for him/her to have made.

One day a black African colleague and I were sent out in a pick-up truck to relieve a similar crew at a fire in a huge mound of tobacco waste that had been dumped on some open ground. (Had I been a smoker, it would have been worth several free packets of untipped.) The other watch and ours had been pumping water onto it for about 48 hours using a street hydrant to feed an old grass-fire appliance, but the water had either run off or evaporated. I told my colleague that we were going to have to dig it out to find the seat of the fire.

"Oh but it is too hot sir", he complained. To be fair, he was the one who would be doing the harder work but hang on a minute: I was supposed to be in charge, so insisted: "Look, if we get stuck in we can be back at the station in a couple of hours to our Sunday afternoon free-time". Sure enough, with his digging and my spraying we soon finished it off and packed the gear away, but I now found myself in something of a quandary. Neither my colleague nor I were HGV drivers in those days, and only the 'front-line appliances' were fitted with a communications radio. We could have waited for more than 2 hours for the next crew to arrive, but that would have brought two men out unnecessarily at the height of the grass fire season and negated all of our hard work. I could have walked (goodness knows how far) to a phone box to request for a driver to be sent out, but knew that to be thought of as 'bloody-minded' or not using one's initiative were considered to be cardinal sins in this particular brigade. So even though I didn't possess an HGV licence, had never driven a lorry before (and this one had a 'crash' gearbox, extremely heavy steering, and appalling brakes) drove it the 7 miles back to the station.   I knew that if it turned out successfully, nothing would be said but fully realised that if it had gone wrong, I would have been in deep, deep dung.

Sometimes it was difficult to remember that we were living in a foreign country, because everyone spoke English and drove on the left. Occasionally I would think I recognised someone I knew but then realise that that person was in fact 6,000 miles away.   Then we'd be dramatically reminded that we did indeed live in the tropics: our garden had a mango tree, chameleons, several ugly and aggressive-looking large spiders; our neighbours grew bananas; my girlfriend awoke one morning to find a deadly Black Mamba snake in her family's swimming pool; and the brother of one of my white colleagues tragically died of malaria.

Then of course the weather was very different from the UK.   Summertime (January to March) was the rainy season and October was known as suicide month because it was so hot and humid, so my favourite time of the year was the winter. There was a slight nip in the air at night and possibly a little frost on the ground first thing in the morning (but certainly not cold enough for an extra pair of shoe-laces), and the temperature during the day would always be in the mid 70s (late 20s centigrade). It would never, ever rain from June to August, so barbecues and picnics could be organised with confidence.

There was a drive-in cinema at a huge site in the suburbs. The rows of concrete humps allowed the drivers to position their cars to face uphill so that the occupants could view the massive screen through the windscreen in comfort. The sound was provided from loudspeakers attached to curly cables and hung from the inside of the car windows, so there were constant reminders to return the speakers to the hook-up posts before driving away, or to hand in any broken ones. Evidently they must have lost many due to those who were too embarrassed to admit their folly. There was a lively party atmosphere during the interval when hamburgers, hot dogs, drinks and ice creams could be purchased. It was all very novel and similar to those scenes we'd seen so often in American films, but we realised that it would have been totally impractical in the British rain, fog and snow.

There was a type of dragonfly with 2 pairs of wings and a plump, white tail section that looked like a huge maggot, which would be attracted into the fire station appliance-room by the lights at night, and then fall stunned to the floor. Each evening the black African firemen would collect them in their hundreds, stuff them into milk-bottles and fry the bodies for their supper. Most of the whites would eat them also, gripping them by the wings while still alive and biting off the juicy body. They would often try to persuade me to sample this delicacy with the assurance that: "They taste like butter". I'm usually quite adventurous with food but always declined this particular offer. "Er, I'll stick with the butter if I forget how it tastes, thanks".

There were so many cultural differences. We heard of a white family who returned from a long holiday abroad to find that their beautiful house had been abused by some black squatters, who had been cooking on an open fire in the middle of the lounge on the polished wooden parquet flooring. Then they found numerous piles of human excrement in the garden, because black Africans believe that white people are uncivilised and disgusting to defecate indoors. I noticed that very few of the black African firemen wore their uniform black socks with the shoes and was told that as they had been brought up without socks, they would sell them for 50 cents to supplement their income.

There was a volleyball court on the station where, because of the weather, we could play almost every day and it was always whites versus blacks. Unlike us, the black Africans didn't take it at all seriously and would pack the court with people which resulted either in 3 men going for the same ball or all of them leaving it to each other. There was a lot of falling over, laughter and banter. I seemed to be alone in finding such one-sided games boring and meaningless, so persuaded an American colleague to privately assist me in hand-picking the best of the blacks and, with some encouragement and basic coaching, taught them to pass the ball, use their superior height and be more aggressive. I don't think they ever won a set of games but they did provide the whites with a much more competitive match.

We were on the court one-day when someone shouted: "Bees!" They all instantly ran for the sanctuary of the appliance room, leaving me behind. I looked up and saw a huge black cloud moving directly overhead, so thought it prudent to catch up with my colleagues where I was told that bees are angered by the sight of waving arms, and that multiple stings have often proved fatal to an unfortunate victim.

The brigade was based on British lines; using the same drill-book, manuals of firemanship, procedures and equipment, but was way behind the times even for those days. There was a lecture room where the theoretical training took place and I noticed that there were some framed sketches on the walls which had been copied from photographs in the manuals (photocopiers were still in their infancy, and scanners hadn't yet been invented). One of these drawings depicted a fireman swinging a large axe and breaking a shop window behind him which was entitled: 'Method of breaking a large window'. I politely pointed out that this was supposed to be a warning about causing unnecessary damage due to carelessness, and not some ludicrous technique for the intentional smashing of a window.

They still used heavy brass and copper fittings that needed to be polished regularly, and today's Health & Safety Executive would have had apoplexy with some of the risks that we accepted. BA safety controls and procedures were non-existent, as people wandered in and out of a fire at will; and there were no BA guidelines, tallies, or emergency safety measures. They still used hook-ladders (3 metres in length with a single serrated arm at the top, used to scale the *outside* of a building from floor to floor, although originally intended for use in narrow streets or alleys) but long since discontinued in Britain as they were deemed to be unnecessary and dangerous. There were also regular carry-down drills using a live 'casualty'; numerous non-standard drills involving the descent of the tower with a friction-reel and sling combination; and various imaginative new opportunities for us to endanger our lives. Unbelievably, one of the black African firemen was always ordered to be the first casualty to test the safety of the procedures and equipment as a human guinea pig. Those who were chosen would be petrified with fear but their desperation to keep such a relatively well paid job would always prevail over their terror.

There was a party of schoolchildren visiting the fire station one-day, and we performed some drills to demonstrate the range of skills that our job entailed. The drill-tower had 2 sets of windows on each of the 6 floors, so I was selected to climb one side to the top and back by hook-ladder while a white colleague, John, was chosen to climb the other side. I should have 'smelled a rat' immediately because John was young, headstrong and extremely competitive. I'd seen him using the hooks on other occasions and been amazed at his flinging himself on and off the ladder like an acrobat, with apparently little regard for his own safety. I'd been taught that it was vital to keep one's weight perpendicular to the centre of the ladder, especially when mounting or dismounting at each window, to prevent the ladder from swinging sideways wildly. (The correct technique is far too complicated and boring to be described here but it involved lots of leaning back into the abyss at arm's-length, to force the lower half of the ladder against the building for stability).

As soon as the order to begin was given, John was off like a rat up a drainpipe as if the devil himself was chasing him with a red-hot poker. I was then horrified to hear the officer urging the children to cheer either for Brian from the UK on the left, or John from Salisbury on the right! It was that patriotic competitiveness again. I doubt whether *anyone* was cheering for me and was too busy concentrating on my technique; climbing safely, steadily and stylishly. In my head, I could hear my old training school instructor's Scouse voice bawling through his megaphone to anyone who was hesitating: "What's the matter lad? Is your a***hole twitching a farthing to a penny?" I could still smile at the hook-ladder memory of the lad on my recruits' course who had mistakenly placed the hook onto the top of an open door, which led to the internal staircase at the top of the tower. This door was slightly above the level of the windowsill so, as he'd begun the ascent from the 5th floor, the door had swung on its hinges taking the ladder away from the building. He'd instantly leapt back into the window from the moving ladder; and was excused any further involvement that day, probably in order for him to change his underwear.

When I reached the ground again, John was crowing that he'd been for a cup of tea while waiting for me to finish the race. (Rhodesia 3 - UK nil).

I replied: "Race? What race? I thought it was a demonstration of the correct and incorrect method of using hook-ladders", gesturing to the left and right.　　　　　　Rhodesia 3 - UK 1.

It was strange that I was unwilling to be left behind by our neighbour on the motorbike, yet my fire brigade training prevented me from risk-taking or corner-cutting when climbing ladders.

The appliances were all British. The P.E. (a pump with a large-wheeled escape ladder on the top) was a 1965 Dennis and the pump was a 1955 Dennis F12, both with Rolls-Royce engines and 'crash' gearboxes, used mainly for property fires and crewed by white personnel with a token black African to do the simple, menial tasks. Then there were four 1950s lorries (Leyland, Bedford, Albion and Austin) in the days when they were limited to 20 mph, locally converted into fire appliances, and used mainly for grass fires, crewed by black Africans but with a white O i/c and one white fireman as his right-hand man.   The Austin pumping appliance – with its chromed 'Flying A' pedestrian slicer emblem on the bonnet -- was an absolute heap of junk.   Its paintwork was faded and dull, the engine was grossly underpowered and the gearing so low that it was all noise with very little forward motion, drowning out the little bell that wouldn't have been out of place on a bicycle. It had a 500 gallon cylindrical water-tank mounted in the style of a tanker, with running-boards along the sides where the crew would stand, hanging on to the handles. We would roar through the town centre at the stately speed of 18mph, with the little bell on the front bumper ting-a-linging, and praying that nobody would recognise us. One day the little hammer in the bell became over-excited and flew off into the long grass at the side of the road, and we actually stopped to look for it. I think it was en route to the same destination, when climbing a long hill; I jumped off the side for a bit of fun, jogged on ahead in full fire-kit, waited for them to catch me up and then casually remounted whilst it was flat-out in third gear.

On another occasion while in full-flight, we were overtaken by a very large black woman on a Velo Solex moped (this was a particularly gutless vehicle, powered (?) by a 29cc engine driving a roller on the front tyre).

On arrival the pump-operator had to crank-up by hand the separate car engine that was mounted on the rear of the appliance and which energised the pump, then crash the gears into mesh with a horrible gnashing of teeth — both human and mechanical -- sending vibrations right up his arm and gradually progressing through every part of his body. I can't believe that I failed to photograph this hideously unique vehicle.

At one of these incidents the fire was in some 10-foot (3m) high elephant grass, with flames nearly as high again. We decided to stop it at a suitable narrow part alongside the road, but I could only stand and watch with the dry hose in my hand as the pump-operator followed his starting-up routine; while the fire roared past us with frightening speed, heat, and sound-effects, disappearing over the hill. The O i/c decided that the fire was heading over the city boundary, so was no longer our problem.

The other vehicles in the line-up were an old Bedford van that had been converted into an ET (emergency tender), and 3 pick-up trucks. A matching pair of these pick-ups was of an obscure Japanese make which were modern, shiny, and very nippy but I always preferred the shabby old Chevy with its large, lazy, yet deceptively fast engine.

There was also an open AEC / Merryweather TL (turntable ladder) of 1934 vintage which always featured in our demonstrations to schoolchildren and other groups visiting the station, so as one of the few British-trained personnel I always felt duty-bound -- much against my better judgement -- to volunteer to be 'shot-up' and swung around at the top of the TL for their entertainment. Looking down from 100 feet and watching in horror as the ladder flexed below me, I couldn't help wondering: Was it suffering from metal fatigue because of its age? Could they obtain the correct spare parts for it, or had they bodged them like everything else there? Were the operators sufficiently trained? Would I ever see home again?

House fire for the other Watch, with the TL in action.

Damping down at the same fire as above.

A recently retired Bedford grass-fire 'appliance'.

Jameson Avenue, which runs through Salisbury. The iconic Pearl Assurance building is in background, statue of Cecil Rhodes is on the central reservation.

Chapter 6.

The winds of change ....

An important aspect of a firefighter's job is to minimise the damage he/she causes with water or breakages. In Rhodesia we regularly failed on both counts, and had a saying -- only half jokingly -- that the result of every fire we attended was either a burnout or it was washed down the Makabusi (river).

I was riding one of the front-line appliances one day when we received a call via the appliance's communications radio to a fire in a bungalow. We weren't far from the address so were the first to arrive at the scene. I noticed that the house was fitted with wrought-iron anti-burglar bars to all of the opening windows, as was the usual practice there, so surmised that Rhodesians would prefer to be burned to death than burgled. (At one such house fire we found the burnt corpse of a man holding the remains of a chair that he had been unsuccessfully using to break out). Anyway this house was heavily smoke-logged, so my BA partner and I donned our breathing apparatus; entered the house with a small-diameter hose reel; located a smouldering mattress in one of the bedrooms and extinguished the fire with the absolute minimum of water or damage just as the second appliance arrived. We couldn't eject the mattress through the window because of the anti-burglar bars, so were folding it up to carry outside when there was a tremendous crash as the huge picture window fell in. Suddenly, ornaments, pictures, and cuddly toys were sent flying in all directions as a large and powerful jet of water drenched the whole room, along with us. "Thanks for coming, lads!"

At another house fire which was dense with thick smoke, one of our crew smashed down what he thought was a locked bedroom door which turned out to be the WC. It transpired that this door wasn't even locked anyway, but merely opened outwards.

On another occasion we were called to a large fire in a single-storey food factory. At one point some cracks appeared in the external walls so we were ordered to evacuate the building. My colleague and I were directing a jet of water through a window into a very large room when one of the managers approached us and pointed to an internal storeroom, which contained some sacks of exotic spices, including saffron worth numerous thousands of dollars in precious foreign currency reserves.

"Please, please, you must try to save it," he

beseeched.   We held the fire back for a couple of hours until we were relieved by another crew, passed on the message about the valuable contents of the store and returned to the station for some food and rest. We returned to the scene a few hours later for damping-down (!) and I was horrified to find the factory completely burnt out, including the store that we'd been fastidiously defending. As I waded knee-deep through the deliciously fragrant 'mud' of assorted potato-crisp flavourings, it occurred to me that we had achieved an unprecedented double, double-whammy of spectacular failure. Not only had we lost most of the contents to fire *and* washed the remainder down the Makabusi; but lost the whole building *and* would be sending the company a huge bill for the benefit of our 'services'. To be fair, we only manned 4 pumps for the whole of the city, and with the nearest brigade being hundreds of miles away if we required assistance, it would have been totally unjust to compare our frugal resources with those of the UK.

Two small stations were then opened in the suburbs; in Greendale at the north side of the city and Waterfalls to the south. Each one housed a Land Rover appliance for the officer and his black African driver, and a lorry converted into a water tender for the black crew. All fire-calls were passed onto us there from the main station by communications radio because there was no phone line fitted.

I was the officer-in-charge at Greendale one day when we received one such call to a fire in the garden of a private house about 5 miles away. Both vehicles normally travelled together because the tender was not equipped with a communications radio, but as the old Albion lorry was so painfully slow I decided to go on ahead and tackle the fire with the Land Rover's 50 gallons of water and hose reel, as I had visions of the whole garden ablaze and threatening the house. I gave the address to the senior black African fireman, showed him where we were going on the wall-map, and dashed off.

The house was typically Rhodesian middle-class, set in huge gardens behind a high hedge, but the fire turned out to be nothing more than a large smouldering compost-heap. We got to work with my driver digging it out and myself spraying the water sparingly, whilst awaiting the arrival of the tender. Occasionally we'd hear the roar of its engine and the graunch of the gears as they toured the district, and once we saw the flashing beacons at the top of a hill in the distance (red beacons for fire appliances, amber for ambulances, and only blue for the police). We must have been there a couple of hours by the time we'd cleared up and taken the details, but still the tender hadn't arrived. As we toured the area looking for them we were flagged-down by a motorist who told us that he'd just found a coil of fire hose at the roadside, and had handed it in to the local police station. The police said that the crew of the tender had called in to ask for directions about an hour previously, so I asked them to keep an eye out for it and send it back to Greendale.

I reluctantly returned to the station to contact the senior officer and confess that I'd lost my fire appliance and crew. He groaned and swore several times. "S***! S***! S***!"

"They're probably in f****** Zambia by now!" I knew not whether his despair was of me, the crew, or the lousy 'hand' that life had dealt him. The tender eventually returned with a police escort after nearly 5 hours, having clocked-up an astonishing 68 miles. I often wonder if the householder was charged for this huge mileage and 5 hours for an appliance and crew, which never even arrived.

On another occasion I was in charge of the Waterfalls station and attending a grass fire that was heading into some elephant-grass on a very large area of open ground. I set the crew to work with beaters, supplemented with hoses from the tender fed from a hydrant, on the upwind side of the fire. Then jumped into the driving-seat of the Land Rover *Firefly* to skirt around the fire so that I could assess whether we needed some assistance from the main station. I was having great fun imagining that I was on safari, and watching the high grass folding down in front of the vehicle, when suddenly the front dropped and it came to a shuddering halt.

I managed to clamber out, with great difficulty, and was mortified to see that the appliance was almost standing on its nose in a 6 feet (2m) deep dried riverbed, at a hideous angle. I panicked on hearing the crackling flames approaching and imagined the photo of the burnt-out shell in the local newspaper, not to mention the fears of my own crispy fate. Even if I'd managed to survive by some miracle, my career probably wouldn't, as this vehicle was priceless and couldn't be replaced because of the international economic sanctions. The Land Rover was equipped with 50 gallons of water and a hose reel which would have been little better than a garden hose when faced with 20 foot high flames. I managed to remount and feverishly engage low-ratio four-wheel-drive, reverse gear, and -- more in desperation than expectation -- applied loads of revs; whereupon the vehicle shot upwards like a champagne cork out of the bottle and briefly became airborne before thudding back onto its wheels. I jarred my spine a little on the frugally upholstered seat but much more importantly; the appliance was completely unscathed apart from some dirt on the front bumper. Chastened, I very cautiously made my escape by following the wheel-tracks and silently pledged my eternal gratitude to those wonderful designers and engineers at the Land Rover factory in faraway Solihull.

We suspected that the Chief Fire Officer had his own communications radio at home and was in the habit of listening in to our operational messages when he was off duty, because he often arrived at an interesting incident without being requested. This was confirmed when I was on watch room duty one Sunday afternoon. In the absence of a phone line at either of the sub stations, one of the officers came in to the watch room to have a 20 minute conversation over the radio with the officer at one of these remote stations, about the skinning, seasoning and cooking of a springbok (that's the small deer, not a South African rugby player). Just as they finished, the distinctive voice of the chief came over the radio, dripping with sarcasm: "A very interesting conversation, and obviously of vital importance to the efficiency of the fire brigade. Over and out!"

One night I was heading for my room when I saw some movement coming out of the A/Ds' dormitory in the dimmed lights of the corridor, followed by one of the ambulance crew. "Did you just see a rat come out of here", he asked breathlessly. "Yes", I replied, "it went that way". We followed it down the corridor, where we found that the only open doors were the Station Officers' & Sub Officers' dormitories. About six of us had assembled by now to form a posse and were wondering which room to search, when we heard a shout and a Stn. O came running out in his `Y` fronts saying that something furry had just run over his face while he was lying in bed. We switched on the lights and started to move the furniture, when the biggest rat I've ever seen came charging out from behind a locker and into the room next door. This procedure was repeated several times until I decided to break the stalemate by taking a broom from a nearby cupboard, and standing guard in the doorway. With its exit now blocked, this Hercules from the rat world started to charge around the room. It really was just like a scene from a comedy film as these big macho men danced about with their trouser legs tucked into their socks, and squealing like girls as the rat ran amongst them. When it saw that I was totally helpless with laughter, it made a dash for the door. My laughter abruptly gagged in my throat and I jabbed at it but missed and it ran past me down the corridor with me in hot pursuit, repeatedly whacking the floor behind it. However, it made the fatal mistake of pausing to run into the A/Ds' room again and I caught it on the back of the head, killing it instantly. Someone picked it up by the tail and dropped it the 30' (10m) out of the window saying that the Africans will eat that. I didn't believe him for a moment, but it had disappeared by morning ……….

One evening some weeks later, I was in the TV room when we heard a commotion in the officers' lounge. We were told that there was another rat in there so we started the furniture-moving routine again, when someone spotted it perched on the doorframe over a door. We were all wondering what to do about it, when a Rhodesian officer strode forward and dispatched it to *Rat Heaven* with a karate chop.

There was always a good chance that our ablutions would be interrupted whilst working a 24 hour shift, and this occurred one day when we were turned-out to a house fire in Harare (which was then the name of the largest of the black African townships) on the outskirts of Salisbury. I was riding the second appliance and donning my fire-kit whilst hanging on grimly as our driver weaved through the rush-hour traffic, which had scattered in response to the urgency of the two-tone air-horns. As we sped through gaps with literally inches to spare, there was a knock on my window. Startled, I looked up to see an upside-down face with shampoo in his hair, who I still recognised as a young white fireman who I shall call Wally, because that really was his name.

"What are you doing there, Wal?" I asked incredulously, as I wound down the window. "I was in the shower when the alarm went-off", he replied, "so I pulled on my skiddies (underpants) and chased the truck down the road (barefoot) and climbed on the back. Anyway never mind all that, pass my fire-kit up". To make matters worse, we were in the middle of a torrential tropical storm with thunder and lightning, so I shouted to the Station Officer in the front seat that Wally was on the roof, but he just shrugged and said nonchalantly: "Well that's his silly fault". So much for Health and Safety! To slightly reduce the risk to Wally, I passed his kit to him through the window, one piece at a time starting with his helmet, obviously. I still laugh out loud when I visualise the reflection in a row of shop windows, of Wally perched on the ladder on top of the appliance as we sped along at 70mph in the lashing rain, and leaning into the wind like a sailing ship's figurehead, with soapsuds still oozing from under his helmet. On arrival, the Africans' house was a raging inferno so, during the couple of hours firefighting and damping-down, poor Wally emitted a cloud of water vapour from his tunic, his normally curly hair was moulded to his head like a Lego man's, and he must have been simmered to perfection.

We had only one TV channel (the RBC) in black and white, but that was more than South Africa had at that time. We received mostly American TV series and films and some British ones. There were also locally produced programmes that were unintentionally hilarious because they were so amateurish. Some of these were versions of British programmes and I first saw *Mastermind*' and *New Faces*' there. The latter used a panel equally critical and cruel as the British one and justifiably so because the talent was almost non-existent. There were comedians with absolutely no originality or charisma relating jokes that might once have amused Adam and Eve, and fluffing the punch lines, or omitting large chunks so that the jokes made no sense. There were singers who assaulted most of the senses, jugglers who dropped things, dancers with very little co-ordination, and technicians who would accidentally walk across the sets in front of the cameras. The slick adverts for the international companies, such as Coca-Cola, were in stark contrast to the locally filmed ones, and in the absence of a Trades' Descriptions Act some outrageous claims were made: "There are now 8 sausages to the pound (!) instead of the usual 6". "Do you need a new (used) car?" (*Everyone* did due to the economic sanctions). "Then come to Joe Bloggs' Car Sales". Then 'Joe' himself would make an appearance, standing in front of the best of his ageing fleet, but whose acting was as wooden as a tree trunk. "Hello, -- I'm -- Joe -- Bloggs. My -- cars -- are -- the -- finest -

- in -- the – coun -- try". Highly debatable, but not saying that much anyway. The ones which amused us most were those depicting white women with hands deep in soapy water and extolling the virtues of a particular brand of liquid soap. Of course very few white women there washed their own dishes or clothes, so as Len queried: "Who on earth would need a house-boy with soft hands?"   Most of the adverts were the screening of a simple card, with a photograph, text and voice-over, but quite often the card would appear with the wrong commentary, or upside-down, whereupon a hand would appear and invert it. The most professional and popular local programme was *Top of the Pops* because it consisted of film clips of British and American pop groups. Gary Glitter's *Hello, Hello, I'm Back Again* was at number 1 in the chart for many weeks because the Rhodesians had never before seen anything like his outrageously 'over-the-top' personality and performance. The black Africans had their own 'Top 20' and their taste in music was generally incomprehensible to us. However, they seemed to identify with Elton John's plaintively evocative song *Daniel*, and they kept it at number 1 in their chart for many months.

I'd often been told how the Rhodesian education system was so much better than the British one but had seen very little evidence of this. For example, I once needed to replace some small batteries in my shaver so called in to the Woolworth's store in the city centre and took 4 loose ones at 11 cents each to the checkout. This was in the days before the standard use of fancy computerised tills, so the young assistant looked up to the ceiling whilst muttering to herself for several seconds. She then wrote the sum of 22 + 22 on a pad before asking for the 44 cents. Whatever happened to times tables and basic mental arithmetic? Next, one of my work colleagues handed out invitations to all of the members of our Watch (well the white ones anyway) for his 21st birthday party at a sports' club. The handwriting was so atrocious, the grammar and spelling so abysmal that the cards were almost illegible and could have been scrawled by a 5 year old; but in the event the birthday boy missed his own party because he had failed to work out the simple equation that we'd all be 'on duty' that weekend. I rest my case.

The station at Waterfalls was situated on a disused campsite in an idyllic setting. The black crewmen occupied the Gents' toilet-block, whilst the O i/c had his office in the Ladies' where he was spoilt-for-choice of showers, hand basins, and WCs. In the evenings I would sit contentedly on the veranda, looking out at the neon lights of the city centre on the horizon, with the warm scented air wrapped around me like a duvet. I would listen to the splashing water that gave the site its name, the chirping of the crickets, the bark of the bullfrogs and various other mysterious sounds of Africa, and wonder how on earth I could ever leave this paradise for the UK. I'd think back to the cold, wet and dirt of Liverpool, of the yobs who would occasionally slash our hoses, throw stones at us or the appliances, and would hitch a ride on the vehicles if we ourselves didn't hang on the back to fend them off until we were well clear of that scene. Their parents didn't seem to know or care where their offspring were at night, but would very swiftly have sued the brigade had their little darlings been injured. However, the "winds of change blowing through Africa" were blowing up to storm-force. The guerrilla war was intensifying in the border areas, and although I was in an exempt occupation and safe from call-up, I could see no long-term future for the country as we knew it. If they had looked at the countries to the north of them, they should have seen that the heavy hand of history was against them. I once inquired about the scabs on a colleague's knuckles, and he casually told me that he and some mates had driven out into the countryside the previous evening and beaten-up a random black man "for a laugh"; whose only mistake was to be born to black African parents, in the right place but at the wrong time. These aggressors apparently couldn't perceive that they were creating resentment and a host of enemies in the unfortunate man, his family, and friends. They were also hastening the end of their privileged and idyllic lifestyle. However, I made some really good friends amongst the white population there and found them to be extremely good company, with a dry and ironic sense of humour. They were also extremely sociable, so enjoyed good, lively house parties but we noticed that the alcohol *always* expired by 10pm, which caused the functions to fizzle out prematurely. The guests either brought a couple of beers and drank ten, or brought more but guzzled as many -- and as quickly -- as humanly possible, to get their share. We were amused to observe that some people secreted bottles in various hiding places for the later stages of the party.

In conversation, they used a peculiar brand of slang with words borrowed from hip American, so that everyone (both male and female) was 'man'; homes were 'pads'; cars were 'cabs'; clothes were 'threads'; meals were 'graze' and thoughts were 'schemes'. They also borrowed words from Afrikaans and native African languages but I couldn't even begin to spell these. To Rhodesians, debt was a way of life, which many of them had absolutely no intention of repaying, yet with a complete absence of worry or shame. We often had bailiffs call at the fire station to reclaim a car, bike, or scooter which had outstanding finance owing on it. Some of my colleagues would show off some expensive watch, camera, or leather jacket that they'd bought on hire purchase and would then abruptly leave the country a few weeks later; presumably taking their illicit possessions with them. Unfortunately, I acquired the reputation as a 'sucker for a sob story'; so on leaving the job was still owed the equivalent of a third of my weekly wage from a large number of people. Each of the Leading Firemen was given an area of responsibility, and mine was hose-repair. The hose-repair room was my little domain where I could talk to the black Africans without being frowned upon. They would bring their shoes in for me to glue their soles back on, and would want to know all about life in Britain. I was surprised to learn of their compulsory education standards and that all blacks (but only the men, I think) were allocated a piece of land in their home village to grow their own crops, but which they didn't actually own, so they couldn't sell or bequeath it to their offspring. Even though I was only treating these black Africans as fellow human beings, I had to be extremely careful to avoid being ostracised by my white colleagues as a 'kaffir-lover'; but was still interested to learn about the Africans' lifestyle so I paid a black colleague a few dollars for an afternoon to show me the best, medium and worst of the houses in their designated areas. However, I felt exceedingly conspicuous as I drove him around because black Africans were usually transported in the rear of pick-up trucks or on the back of a lorry and very rarely in the front passenger seat, so I also felt inexplicably guilty and fearful of being recognised by someone. Some of the houses and flats in the townships were indeed grim, as were the mud huts in the villages; but a few of the houses were far more luxurious than many white people would ever be able to afford.

I had attended a half-day course on hose-repair during my service in Liverpool, so could jokingly boast that I was probably the foremost authority with regard to hose-repair in the whole of Rhodesia. It was much easier to be a *somebody* in a relatively small country. For example: Ed, Len, their Rhodesian fiancées, and I were invited to the high-society wedding of the daughter of some friends we had made there and I'd spent the afternoon and evening in the delightful company of a beautiful and vivacious young lady to whom I'd just been introduced. At the culmination of the evening she gave me her phone number because it was ex-directory, due to her father's occupation as a civil servant. The next day our friends revealed that her father was actually David Smith, the Rhodesian

Chancellor of the Exchequer (no relation to Premier Ian Smith, as far as I'm aware). I would have dearly loved to see her again but had already booked my return journey home and didn't need any more complication in my life. We'd met a lot of families there who had repeatedly shuttled between the UK, Rhodesia, South Africa, and Australia, only to find themselves in a sort of nomadic limbo, fruitlessly searching for an elusive Utopia. It appeared that some people only remember the good aspects of their previous homelands but none of the drawbacks, seemingly doomed to never learn that the perfect country doesn't exist.

It was now late in 1973 and I had spent two Christmases away from my family, so was determined to be home for the next. I took it as a compliment that many of the black Africans were sorry to hear of my impending departure. "But we like you here", they said, as if that were sufficient reason for me to stay.

The aspects of Britain I was surprised that I

missed the most -- apart from decent television programmes, proper professional football matches, pubs, family and friends, obviously -- were the uniquely British sporting occasions, such as Wembley cup finals, Wimbledon tennis, the Grand National horse race, University Boat Race, and the Isle-of-Man TT motorcycle races. There are also no foreign equivalents of our Remembrance Sunday, Royal Tournament, Last Night of the Proms, Edinburgh Tattoo, Guy Fawkes' Night, Royal weddings and funerals, etc.

Ed and Len were called-up by the army several times but managed to get it deferred for a few months. Len eventually flew home with his Rhodesian fiancée, but they have since married and returned to live in South Africa. Ed stayed on, married a local girl, served several tours of duty dodging the land mines with the army during the bush war, and returned to the UK, but they now live in Australia.

I flew to Johannesburg, caught the famous

Blue Train sleeper for the 3 day journey to Cape Town and boarded the MV *Windsor Castle*. I needed to kill a few hours before sailing, so decided to do some last minute shopping. I was waiting at a bus stop when I became aware of people staring at me from the passing traffic, some gesticulating. I checked my zip. OK. Perhaps they'd mistaken me for somebody famous. Then an elderly gentleman of mixed race joined me. "Excuse me sir, but are you waiting for a bus?" he inquired. I affirmed that I was. "Then you must wait at the stop along there"; he pointed to another stop 30 yards away. "This is only for non-white people". Both buses would be following the same route to the very same destination. No change there then, but it did remove any lingering doubts that I might have harboured about leaving that continent. I left the heat of an African summer for the cold and wet of a British winter, which at the time was suffering from petrol rationing, power-cuts, a 3-day working week due to the miners' strikes; and the Irish nationalists were extending their bombing campaign to the British mainland. The singer, Leo Sayer, was appearing on TV, dressed as a clown and singing '*I Won't Let the Show Go On*'; and the members of a pop group were dressed in furry costumes, pretending to play musical instruments and singing about picking up litter on Wimbledon Common. I wondered what on earth I'd come back to! Sleepy, staid, old-fashioned Rhodesia suddenly seemed to be far more civilised, and somewhere to which I could far more relate.

I eventually joined a British brigade again, and married a beautiful Worcestershire girl who has given me two wonderful daughters. I went on to serve 25 years as a firefighter in Kidderminster, then a further 10 years of servicing breathing apparatus for the same brigade in the glorious counties of Herefordshire and Worcestershire; so in moments of contemplation, I sometimes shudder when I remember how I so **very** nearly declined the greatest adventure -- and turning point of my life.

The small fire station at Greendale.

The crew at Waterfalls. (There was one other who declined to be photographed as he believed his soul would be trapped in the camera.)

Waterfalls crew in fire kit.

An African village.

African villagers.

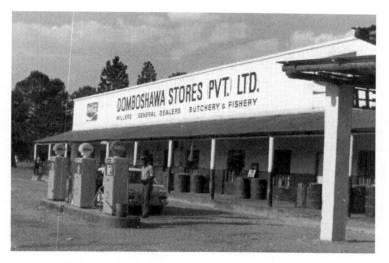

Rural general store with petrol station.

One of the townships.

Africans' houses in one of the townships.

An African single men's hostel in a township.

African beer garden. The cycling African has a gallon takeaway.

Len & Ed with our girlfriends in a hotel garden. How could we ever leave this paradise?

<u>Epilogue.</u>

We took a holiday in South Africa in 2004 so that I could show my wife some of the region of which I've often spoken and which still holds a large piece of my heart. We spent a few days with Len and his family in their beautiful home in Port Elizabeth, which would have been worth at least 10 times its current value if only it could have been transplanted into the UK.

I was amazed by the changes that had taken place in the country since I was last there, mainly due to Nelson Mandela's policies of forgiveness and reconciliation, along with Affirmative Action (positive discrimination). Black and mixed-race people are now employed in positions of responsibility, whereas many white people are often reduced to accepting menial jobs, or self-employment such as the guarding of people's cars outside theatres or restaurants until late at night. One of Len's sons was expected to live only on the tips from his job as a waiter. In fact, not only did the restaurant owner not pay any wages whatsoever but he also confiscated some of the tips to cover breakages, just in case. The racial groups all seemed to have integrated harmoniously however. The nostalgic Zimbabwe holiday of Ed and family in the early Nineties was not so encouraging though. After several years away, they were shocked to witness this once-prosperous country spiralling into disastrous decline, with a marked collapse in the living standards of *every* racial group apart from the black politicians, their families and their cronies. Most of the shops' shelves were empty; there were huge queues for petrol; and the infrastructure was in an advanced state of decay, with lifts, escalators, and other machinery failing to be repaired after breaking down. On checking-in to the 5* Meikles hotel in the centre of Harare (see photo in chapter 4) they were ordered to tip their suitcases out onto the floor of the reception where a black security guard rummaged through the pile of possessions. He was particularly interested in their camcorder, which were very rare there in those days. Their room was fabulous, with a balcony overlooking Cecil Square (named after Cecil Rhodes) and they were amused to see that the founding fathers of the city had planted red, white, and blue flowering trees all over the garden in the square to produce one of the world's largest Union Flags, but which could only be appreciated when seen from above. The significance of this had obviously escaped the notice of Robert Mugabe and his government at that time!

Unfortunately Ed's room also overlooked some government buildings which bristled with antennas and satellite dishes so, just as they were settling in, were abruptly moved to another room at the rear of the hotel on some flimsy pretext. The view from this room was terrible and the hotel horrendously expensive, so they moved to another one after a few days where the suitcase ritual was repeated. This security guard then said: "Ah, you're the man with the video camera!" Ed's notoriety had apparently been broadcast over the 'jungle drums'. Whilst having a drink in the hotel lounge each evening, it became obvious to Ed, his wife, and some old Rhodesian friends who kept arriving to meet them, that they were under constant surveillance by a black African man in a smart, expensive suit who sat at the adjoining table even though every other table was unoccupied in this huge room; but whenever they glanced across at him he'd quickly and amateurishly pretend to be reading his newspaper. This eavesdropper was replaced by another on a regular basis in a bid to avert suspicion, except that he and his colleagues seemed to consider it normal for a succession of people to use the same newspaper – and to sip from the same glass.

Reunited with Ed & Len in Australia 2014.
The first time we've all been together for 41 years.

Acknowledgements.

I must thank several people for their assistance to me in writing this book:-

My wife, Jill, for her patience and tolerance.

My sons-in-law, Mark and Andy, for their computer expertise.

Lastly but certainly not least -- my good mates, Ed and Len, for helping my memory with some of the details, and of course inviting me along on this great adventure which ultimately altered the direction of each of our lives, irrefutably for the better.

If you've enjoyed this book, I'd be very grateful if you could 'like' it on the Facebook page below. Thanks, Brian.

https://www.facebook.com/pages/My-passage-to-Africa/294207894007048

or post a review on Amazon at:-
www.amazon.co.uk/product-reviews/B005W37XF0

Printed in Great Britain
by Amazon